THE LITTLE BOOK

OF
EMERGING
MARKETS

Little Book Big Profits Series

In the *Little Book Big Profits* series, the brightest icons in the financial world write on topics that range from tried-and-true investment strategies to tomorrow's new trends. Each book offers a unique perspective on investing, allowing the reader to pick and choose from the very best in investment advice today.

Books in the *Little Book Big Profits* series include:

THE LITTLE BOOK

OF

EMERGING MARKETS

How to Make Money in the World's Fastest Growing Markets

MARK MOBIUS

WILEY

John Wiley & Sons Singapore Pte. Ltd.

Copyright © 2012 by Mark Mobius.

Published by John Wiley & Sons Singapore Pte. Ltd.
1 Fusionopolis Walk, #07-01, Solaris South Tower, Singapore 138628

All rights reserved.

No part of this publication may be reproduced, stored in a retrieval system, or transmitted in any form
or by any means, electronic, mechanical, photocopying, recording, scanning, or otherwise, except as
expressly permitted by law, without either the prior written permission of the Publisher, or authorization
through payment of the appropriate photocopy fee to the Copyright Clearance Center. Requests for
permission should be addressed to the Publisher, John Wiley & Sons Singapore Pte. Ltd.,
1 Fusionopolis Walk, #07-01, Solaris South Tower, Singapore 138628, tel: 65-6643-8000,
fax: 65-6643-8008, e-mail: enquiry@wiley.com.

This publication is designed to provide accurate and authoritative information in regard to the subject
matter covered. It is sold with the understanding that the Publisher is not engaged in rendering professional services. If professional advice or other expert assistance is required, the services of a competent
professional person should be sought. Neither the author nor the Publisher is liable for any actions
prompted or caused by the information presented in this book. Any views expressed herein are those of
the author and do not represent the views of the organizations he works for.

Other Wiley Editorial Offices

John Wiley & Sons, 111 River Street, Hoboken, NJ 07030, USA

John Wiley & Sons, The Atrium, Southern Gate, Chichester, West Sussex, P019 8SQ,
    United Kingdom

John Wiley & Sons (Canada) Ltd., 5353 Dundas Street West, Suite 400, Toronto, Ontario,
    M9B 6HB, Canada

John Wiley & Sons Australia Ltd., 42 McDougall Street, Milton, Queensland 4064, Australia

Wiley-VCH, Boschstrasse 12, D-69469 Weinheim, Germany

ISBN 978-1-118-15381-9 (Hardcover)
ISBN 978-1-118-15370-3 (ePDF)
ISBN 978-1-118-15382-6 (Mobi)
ISBN 978-1-118-15383-3 (ePub)

Typeset in 12.75/15.5, CgCloister by MPS Limited, Chennai, India
Printed in Singapore by Markono Print Media Pte. Ltd.

10 9 8 7 6 5 4 3 2 1

To my mother and father
for giving me
the opportunity to learn

Contents

Chapter Nine
**It's Called Volatility: What Goes
Up Comes Down, and What Goes
Down Comes Back Up**

Chapter Ten
**The Importance of Being Contrary:
Don't Follow the Crowd**

Chapter Eleven
**The Big Picture and the Small Picture:
A Case Study of Russia**

Field Note: Russia

Chapter Twelve
**Pri·va·ti·za·tion: The Trend That
Can Bring Huge Opportunities**

Chapter Thirteen
Boom to Bust: How, When, and Why?

Chapter Fourteen
**Don't Get Emotional: How to Profit
from the Panic**

Introduction

———— ❧ ————

ONE OF THE MOST frequent questions I get asked is: "When's the best time to invest?" The answer is: The best time to invest is when you have money. The reality is that market timing is impossible, and since purchasing ordinary shares of companies traded on a stock exchange (which is called equity investing) is the best way to preserve value, rather than leaving money in a bank account, it is most advisable to just get going. Don't wait for the fabled perfect moment. That answers the question of when to buy, but what about knowing when to sell? My advice on that issue is that an investment should not be sold unless a much better investment has been found to replace it.

"The best time to invest is when you have money."

—*Sir John Templeton*

To me, more important than the question of *when* to invest is the question of *where* to invest. My bias rests with emerging markets. Emerging markets are the financial markets of economies that are in the growth stage of their development cycle and have low to middle per capita incomes. The opposite of an emerging market is a developed market, the financial market of a mature economy with a high per capita income.

Emerging markets possess a greater upside in the long term because of their strong economic growth. Specifically, they offer the best opportunity for higher returns and diversification. It might also surprise you to know that emerging economies account for about two-thirds of the world's land mass—that's a large part of the world that you can't afford to miss out on!

Emerging markets are close to my heart; having worked in emerging countries for more than 40 years, I've learned a great deal about how their markets work and where money can be made. This book not only introduces you to emerging markets, but also describes where, why, and how you can invest in them. I also give you insights into individual markets and some of the crises that these markets have withstood; I hope to equip you with information that will help you better navigate through your search for investments in these markets.

But while we're on the topic of when, I'd like to share something I've learned over the years: Bull markets run longer and gain more in percentage terms than bear markets, which last a short period of time and fall less in percentage terms. This is an important overall phenomenon of which to be aware, because it is a factor when deciding whether to invest.

Market timing is difficult, but it is generally safe to assume that a bull market is coming eventually and that the stock market will rise above its previous highs during that time. Moreover, if you're strong enough to hold your own in both up and down markets, the best thing to do is to buy more stocks when the bear market comes, because it is going to be shorter in duration than the bull market. Investors who bought during the last bear market in 2008, for example, in many emerging markets doubled their money. Of course we'll have more bear markets going forward, but the lesson is clear.

Before diving in, let's look at an example. In January 1988, a bull market run in emerging markets began that lasted for about nine and a half years and saw the index climb over 600% from its starting point. The ensuing bear market lasted just over a year and saw a loss of more than 50% in the value of the index. The next bull market began in September 1998, and over the course of a year and a half, gained over 110% in value. This was followed by a similar-duration bear run in which prices declined by close to 50%.

The point is clear, and can be demonstrated again from October 2001 to November 2007, when the bull market returned more than 530% in just over six years,

The Ups and Downs (but Mostly Ups) of the MSCI Emerging Markets Index

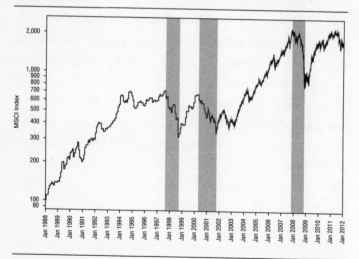

Note: Bear market based on 30% decline from the peak and bull market based on 30% increase from the bottom.

and was followed by a bear market that lost 65% in the subsequent 12 months.

Throughout the book you'll find Field Notes from my recent trips to countries considered to have emerging or frontier equity markets. These notes highlight industries to watch for and offer a glimpse into the sentiment there.

While there is no simple secret, blueprint, or road map to guarantee long-term success in emerging markets, there are plenty of good, solid lessons such as diversification, taking a long-term view, focusing on fundamentals, and tolerating market volatility. These lessons and more are what I have tried to put together in this book. I only hope that this Little Book can be your guide to big profits in emerging markets.

Author's Disclaimer

―――――――――――― ∽ ――――――――――――

THE VIEWS EXPRESSED IN this book are solely my own, and do not necessarily represent the views of my employer.

The opinions expressed should not be relied upon as investment advice or an offer for a particular security. These opinions and insights may help you understand our investment management philosophy.

Statements of fact included in this book are from sources considered reliable, but the author makes no representation or warranty as to their completeness or accuracy.

Chapter One

What Are Emerging Markets?

~

An Investment Opportunity Not to Be Missed

WHILE I WAS STUDYING economic development at MIT in the early 1960s, the term *underdeveloped countries* was still in use, while more palatable euphemisms like *developing countries* were just coming into being.

The term *emerging markets* entered the vocabulary of the investment world in the late 1980s. The International

Finance Corporation defined an emerging market this way: "A market growing in size and sophistication in contrast to a market that is relatively small, inactive, and gives little appearance of change." At the time, the term was a declaration of hope and faith on the part of those of us who were studying emerging stock markets, because many of these markets—such as those of Argentina, Peru, and Venezuela—were submerging faster than they were emerging.

The Name of the Game

The purview of international portfolio investors was quite limited in the early days. In fact, if the concept of emerging markets had been current at that time, Japan would probably have been placed in that category. In the 1960s, investing in Japan was considered to be a risky and pioneering adventure; it was known as a land of cheap and shoddy exports, weak currency, and an unstable political future.

When Sir John Templeton asked me to manage the first emerging markets fund in 1987, a universally accepted operational definition of an emerging market did not exist. Intuitively it was known that *emerging* implied developing or underdeveloped, but it wasn't possible to ascertain what the cutting-off point for "emerging" versus "emerged" markets would be. However, the World

Bank's classification of "high-income," "middle-income," and "low-income" countries on the basis of per capita income was a good start. The middle- and low-income countries were considered to be "emerging."

Since 1987, when that original list of emerging markets was compiled from World Bank data, there have been a number of changes in the per capita income rankings of countries, with countries moving into new categories.

For example, the matter of countries with huge natural resources in the developing world, particularly in the Middle East, had to be addressed. While these countries clearly could not be classified as developed because of the low levels of infrastructure and income distribution at that time, they often had high per capita income levels due to the strong exports of resources such as oil and gas. Thus, although such countries as Qatar and Kuwait had per capita incomes significantly higher than the low- and middle-income countries, the distribution of that income was such that general living standards had not reached developed country status.

Some of the emerging country stock markets are well developed and are considered by some international investors as not belonging to the emerging country category. For example, Hong Kong is considered by a number of international investors as one of the world's major stock markets and therefore is not included in their lists of emerging markets. One pension fund manager said, "I don't consider Hong Kong an emerging market because it's easy to invest there and it's very liquid." However, when you consider the fact that Hong Kong is part of China, which is in the middle per capita income category, it is clearly in the emerging country category. Another important factor that needs to be taken into consideration is that in the case of many of the listed companies in Hong Kong, a large part of their earnings are generated in China; thus it would be mistake not to include those opportunities in the emerging market category.

Emerging markets are the financial markets of economies that are in the growth stage of their development cycle and have low to middle per capita incomes.

Emerging, Emerging, Emerged!

Another question: When does a stock market cease to be an emerging market? As emerging country income levels rise and emerging stock markets become more developed and easily accessible to all international investors, we then face the challenge of deciding which countries or markets should be deleted from the list and which should be added. For example, there has been much talk of whether South Korea and Taiwan should graduate to the status of developed markets.

The emerging markets list will continue to change as economic and political situations evolve around the globe. For now, though, emerging market countries are considered to include those classified to be developing or emerging by the World Bank, the International Finance Corporation, the United Nations, or the countries' authorities, as well as countries with a stock market capitalization of less than 3% of the MSCI World index. These countries are typically located in Asia (excluding Japan), the Middle East, Eastern Europe, Central and South America, and Africa. Of all the markets, about 170 countries meet these conditions today.

At first glance, it may seem that the range of countries is prohibitively diverse for serious investment analysis. But there were, and still are, practical factors that serve to reduce the list for investors. Many countries were excluded as initial investment possibilities because of a number of barriers, such as foreign investment restrictions, taxation, and the lack of stock markets. Gradually more and more countries finally abandoned the socialist/communist economic model and came to realize that a market economy would yield faster growth. This resulted in both bond and stock markets becoming open to foreign investors in addition to local investors. By opening up their markets to foreign investors, countries allow investors living outside of their borders to invest in their stock markets and thus attract more capital as they become more integrated to the larger global markets.

The FELT Criteria

Even though markets are more accessible now, some barriers remain. Before I'm willing to enter any stock market, I would like it to have some minimum requirements that I've defined by an easy acronym: FELT. It stands for:

- *Fair:* Are all investors treated equally? Does the company have one class of shares so that each share has equal voting rights? Is market information available to all investors?
- *Efficient:* Can investors buy and sell shares easily and safely? Are the systems for keeping track of trades rapid and accurate with a minimum of delays so that money is not tied up unnecessarily?
- *Liquid:* Is there sufficient turnover or volume to be able to freely buy and sell shares in the market? Is the free float, or number of shares normally available for trading, a high percentage of the total number of shares outstanding?

- *Transparent:* Is it easy to find out what's really going on in this market? Am I able to obtain information from the listed companies? Do they publish audited financial statements?

If a market meets the FELT criteria, you can get excited about it. If it doesn't, approach with great care.

In fact, when I started investing in emerging markets for Templeton in 1987, there were just a handful of markets to invest in at the time. Of course, before entering a new market there were many administrative and technical details to surmount, such as establishing a custodial bank to keep our securities safe, studying the local laws and regulations, learning about the complexities of the specific country's trading systems, and many other details in addition to the main task of learning about the possible company investments. Over the years, the emerging markets investable universe went from only five stock markets in 1987 to over 60 today.

Top Reasons for Investing in Emerging Markets

Growth and Diversification

WHY INVEST IN EMERGING markets? Because that's where the growth is!

Economies of emerging markets are growing much faster than those of higher-income, developed countries. The International Monetary Fund (IMF) estimated that emerging economies would grow by 6% in 2012, three times faster than the 2% growth estimated for developed countries.

Why the Sudden Growth Spurt?

What are the reasons for this uptick in emerging market growth? When a country is growing at 5% and the population is growing at only 1%, then the per capita income increases at a fast rate. This is what is happening in emerging markets. This fundamental development is enhanced by another high growth propellant: the relatively low base from which these nations have been emerging, which allows for spectacular jumps in growth.

Emerging market countries are also in luck in this critical sense: They have not had to reinvent the wheel—the cell phone, the laser printer, or industrial robots—to realize the rewards of modern technology. In practical terms, for example, this means that some countries were able to establish stock exchanges that didn't need trading floors, because all trading was electronic and brokers could enter buy and sell orders using computers. The productivity enhancements gained by technological innovations could be obtained in the blink of an eye. Such technology transfers have helped propel growth in emerging markets.

Moreover, with inevitable shortages of almost every service and commodity and an unfulfilled demand for new products as the wealth of the emerging nations grows, the opportunities for businesses can be unprecedented. As spending in those economies increases and the requirements for credit and finance expand, capital and equity market developments are stimulated.

In China, for example, only 1% of rural households had refrigerators in 1990. As living standards and incomes increased over the years, this number shot up to 37% in 2009. Similarly, only 9% had washing machines in 1990, compared to more than 50% in 2009. Only 7% of rural households in China had computers in 2009. This is pale compared to developed countries such as the United States, where close to 70% of households had Internet access at home by 2009. Clearly, the potential for further growth is huge.

Stock markets in emerging countries are flourishing in tandem with economic growth. Stock market expansion allows for greater movement in stock values. These moves can be up or down, but in light of tremendous economic expansion, they are largely expected to continue rising. As more companies find themselves in a position to go public or are privatized by the state sector, there is a greater range of companies to choose from, in significant sectors of the economy like energy, finance, and industry. In 2011, for example, initial public offerings (IPOs) and follow-on issues exceeded US$245 billion, about 30% more than that recorded in the U.S. market and about 40% of the global total. The numbers were even more significant in 2010, when IPOs and follow-on issues in emerging markets totaled US$470 billion, more than double the US$198 billion recorded in the U.S. market and about half the world's US$950 billion.

By 2011, emerging markets represented 34% of the total world's stock market capitalization compared to less than 10% 10 years before. These statistics may be shocking to many longtime investors who are accustomed to thinking only about developed markets, but they mean that investors today have many more choices and ways to expose their portfolios to these high-growth emerging markets than any of us did 20, 10, or even 5 years ago.

Investing in emerging markets in particular enhances the performance contribution or benefits of diversification, since emerging markets have generally performed better than the developed markets. Since 1988, one year after we launched the Templeton Emerging Markets Fund, the accompanying chart shows that emerging markets have outperformed the U.S. market by about 940% and the world market by more than 1,360% as of the end of January 2012.

Emerging Markets Performance versus the World and U.S. Markets

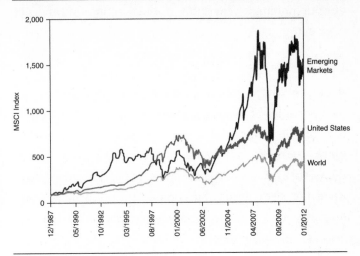

Data source: MSCI, FactSet.

Of course, from one year to the next performance will vary and in some years emerging markets will underperform other markets, but in most years emerging markets are the winners. There can be dramatic differences between various countries. For example, in 2010, Argentina and Sri Lanka returned in excess of 70% in U.S. Dollar terms, while on the other end of the spectrum Bahrain and Kazakhstan saw declines of 18% and close to 15% in U.S. Dollar terms. It is thus logical that if you have investments spread across a number of countries, you have a better chance of at least a portion of your holdings generating optimal returns during any one year.

A "Problem" of Too Many Choices

Whether you're thinking about putting together your own portfolio of emerging markets stocks or buying into one of the many global or emerging markets mutual funds, a critical first step is to take a long, hard look at the world. You may not have done this at any great length since the sixth grade, but time spent studying a world map can never be wasted, and can be critical to your success as a global investor.

The first thing you'll probably notice is the relatively small size of the developed markets compared to the vast swaths of land covering the emerging countries. Emerging economies cover 77% of the world's land mass, have more than 80% of the world's population, hold more than 65% of the world's foreign exchange reserves, and account for about 50% of the world's gross domestic product (GDP). In 2010, about 5.7 billion people resided in emerging countries; that's about five times the 1.2 billion population of the developed markets. China and India alone account for more than 2.5 billion people; that's almost four times the approximately 700 million in the United States and European Union.

Within the emerging markets asset class, one could easily differentiate between the more mature or well-known emerging markets and the frontier markets, which are those that are younger and less developed.

Markets such as Brazil, Hong Kong, and India could be considered to be *mature* emerging markets not because they are immune to the volatility common to all emerging markets but because they offer a wide range of investment opportunities, some degree of transparency in the operation of their markets, and comparatively advanced systems of investor protection, including securities regulation and treatment of minority shareholders. These markets also have a more robust and developed local investor base, and have become less susceptible to the rise and fall of foreign risk appetite.

These nations comprise key markets in emerging market portfolios and should be examined closely for opportunities by any prospective emerging markets investor with the time to do the in-depth study.

Of course, frontier markets such as Nigeria, Vietnam, and Pakistan can be places to make substantial profits because the perception by the investing public is that those places are more "risky" and thus are avoided. This attitude often means that prices are low and the opportunity to obtain cheap stocks is good. This brings us right to this truth: Taking risks is the best way investors can make profits.

---~---

**Taking risks is best way investors
can make profits.**

Today, China, India, Indonesia, Brazil, and Russia
(known as the Big Five) are all viable emerging markets,
by anyone's yardstick. Not only are they emerging, but
all are among the world's 20 largest economies, with
China, Brazil, and India in the top 10. These economies
are clearly economic powerhouses of the twenty-first
century.

Let's take a quick look at that list again: China, India,
Indonesia, Brazil, and Russia. In the 1990s, all five could
have easily wound up on a list of the world's financial disaster zones. But today, the Economist Intelligence Unit fore-
casts that growth in these rapidly emerging countries will
surge an average of 6.5% a year through 2020, beating
by a wide margin the comparatively tepid performance of
the 1.9% growth rate by the developed economies. But,
of course, the crash in Indonesia and other Asian countries in 1997 and 1998, as well as the economic collapse of
Russia in mid-1998, proved that real dangers remain.

The prominence of these emerging market nations
has changed the economic map of the world over the past

25 years. So what does that mean for you, the aspiring global investor—or for me, for that matter?

All five economic powerhouses should be places you should be taking a closer look at to see if you can find companies in them you'd like to invest in. Apart from the Big Five, the high growth rates enjoyed by nearly all emerging markets today (of course there are exceptions) suggest the following: If you want to gain exposure to the world's fastest-growing economies, you've got to take the plunge into emerging stock markets. Why? It's all about GROWTH!

All Markets Are Volatile Sometimes

Between 2000 and 2010, the economies of four major emerging markets—Brazil, Russia, India, and China, commonly known as the BRIC markets, grew by 112%. Over the same period, the economies of three major advanced countries—the United States, the United Kingdom, and Japan—grew by a comparatively insipid 14%.

In 2000, the average gross domestic product (GDP) growth of the world's emerging market countries hovered around 6.5%. At the same time, the average growth of the developed countries was a little under 4%.

A decade later in 2010, the growth gap between the world's emerging and developed markets had widened even further: The emerging markets average was 7.7% but the developed markets average was just 2.6%.

Take note: These stupendous growth rates should not be taken as proof that stock markets in the emerging markets will continue to appreciate substantially in tandem with their high-growth economies.

If anything, the Asian contagion of 1997 to 1998, much like the Latin American "tequila effect" of three years before, demonstrates that emerging markets have not been immune to shocks and are liable to take a few tumbles and stumbles on the road to wealth and prosperity. However, it's that very volatility that, if managed appropriately, can generate well above average returns over the long haul.

We've all got to face up to the fact that volatility is a characteristic in all markets—even the most mature ones.

Volatility is a characteristic in all markets— even the most mature ones.

The reason for this is really quite simple: All markets, being based more in mass psychology than objective reality, have a tendency to overshoot and undershoot economic growth rates. Judging the influence of irrational emotion is, by the way, the way patient investors can make money.

If you factor emotion out of the equation and base your strategy on long-term fundamentals, you can win both when markets fall and when markets rise.

Such overshootings and undershootings tend to cancel each other out over time, by the way. This means that stock markets do eventually reflect economic growth in the long haul. But also like all markets, emerging markets tend to be cyclical. That's a nice way of saying that sometimes they go boom, and sometimes they go bust.

The best way to take the edge off this volatility, I've found, is to faithfully follow the time-honored value-oriented and sometimes contrarian strategy first pioneered by our mentor, the late Sir John Templeton, often called the godfather of global investing. Sir John Templeton was a pioneer in financial investment and was among the first investors to venture into Japan in the 1960s, when it was still known as an underdeveloped economy. His strategy was to:

- Search the world for the best investment bargains.
- Focus on the long term, not the short term.
- Use common sense.

When we see unrecognized value, we are willing to be contrarian, buying when others are despondently selling, and selling when others are greedily buying.

The great paradox of value investing is that most of the money is made after—as opposed to before—the fall. Whether it's the Asian contagion, the Latin American tequila effect, or the U.S. subprime crisis, it's important to keep in mind that you're going to find the most and the best bargains during hard times, when the news is bad and when everyone else wants to sell.

Bad times can be good times. Or, as a colleague of mine once put it: "For us, bad news is good news."

In addition to increasing the probability of recording higher returns by diversifying investments among many countries instead of just one, portfolios tend to be less volatile because of the wider diversity of holdings and broader range of economic and political variables affecting the investments.

When I started out in emerging markets, with only around US$100 million in the kitty (in contrast to more than US$50 billion today), only a handful of countries met our investment criteria. Of those, tiny Hong Kong—where I'd lived in my early investing days—was our pivot, our linchpin.

I knew, or imagined I knew, the practices and characteristics of Hong Kong's market and the behavior of Chinese investors there and felt safe. But when we first began investing heavily in the Hong Kong market in October 1987, the great U.S. stock market crash was just sending shock waves around the world, bringing down world markets, many of which were just starting to recover from the 1970s slump brought on by the global oil crisis.

When the tidal wave hit Asia, the head of the Hong Kong Stock Exchange closed the market down for three days. By the time it reopened, we had paper losses of roughly a third of our total portfolio value. This profoundly unsettling experience (which featured me personally persuading many spooked investors to sit tight and ride out the wave) taught me and my then-tiny emerging markets team an unforgettable lesson about the inherent risk of putting too many eggs in one basket. I learned that it was actually possible to have all your eggs in the wrong basket at the wrong time.

This traumatic financial upheaval drove home—like a nail—one of the most important rules of investing in emerging markets: Your best protection is diversification.

Your Best Protection Is Diversification

To reduce one's vulnerability to a severe downturn in one market, every investor should diversify. That is your best protection against unexpected events, natural disasters, and dishonest management, as well as investor panic. Moreover, global investing across all sectors is always superior to investing in only one market or industry.

If you search worldwide, you will find more bargains and better bargains than by studying only one market. You never want to be overly dependent on the fate of any one stock, market, or sector.

Diversification of assets among many countries and many stocks leads to lower volatility and lower risk, without limiting the potential for gain. This is because there is a broader range of influencing economic and political variables to impact your investments in different ways in different countries. A simple example is when oil prices are high, companies in oil-exporting countries like Russia or the United Arab Emirates will have more profitable returns and will generate a better performance while companies depending on imported oil power in oil-importing countries, like Japan, may turn in weaker results and experience a drop in their share prices.

If U.S. investors diversify from their U.S. holdings by making investments only in, say, the United Kingdom, the diversification effect exists, but not as markedly as if the investor moved into markets such as Bahrain, Jordan, Bangladesh, and Slovenia. This is because the correlation coefficient, or ratio of times in which the markets move in tandem, of the UK stock market indexes to the U.S. indexes have been found to be as high as 0.98 out of a total maximum of 1.0. This means that 9.8 times out of 10, when the U.S. markets are weak, so are the UK markets. For emerging markets, the numbers are lower. In the end, a given portfolio has benefited from only a minor degree of diversification and risk reduction. In contrast, Bahrain, Jordan, Bangladesh, and Slovenia all have a negative correlation to the United States, which means that when the U.S. market falls, these markets may actually rise, and vice versa. Emerging and frontier market investments therefore serve to reduce the risk of volatility in a portfolio to a much greater extent than investments in other developed markets would.

The potential for gain also exists between two different emerging and frontier markets. Even individual markets can move quite independently of each other, providing a great advantage to a diversified portfolio over single-country investments. In some years, there has been a correlation coefficient of only 0.28 between the Thailand and Egypt markets, and 0.32 between Turkey and Nigeria. China and Jordan actually have had a negative correlation, as have South Korea and Bahrain. Therefore, a portfolio with a selection of emerging market stocks, rather than a portfolio with one emerging market and one developed market, is likely to gain greater diversification benefits.

Of course, as the world gets smaller, as communications become better and faster and as global investors invest more in the emerging markets, the correlation between the developed and the emerging markets has drawn closer together. This is especially the case in times of crisis, and was evident during the U.S. subprime crisis in 2008, the Asian financial crisis in 1998, and even the Mexican Peso devaluation in 1994.

Fortunately, diversification has become easier with more opportunities to choose from. Today there are many more baskets and far fewer basket cases. In 1987, when Templeton launched the first listed emerging markets mutual funds on the New York Stock Exchange, no other U.S.-based mutual funds invested significant portions of their portfolios overseas. But today investors have access to more than 6,000 equity funds that invest in emerging markets.

In addition to growing at much faster rates than developed countries, emerging economies are becoming stronger and more immune to external shocks than they were in the late 1990s. Emerging countries tend to have higher foreign exchange reserves and lower debt levels than their developed counterparts.

As of August 2011, emerging markets as a group had about US$7,000 billion in total reserves (excluding gold), double the approximately US$3,500 billion in developed markets. In comparison, the world's largest foreign exchange reserve holder, China had more than US$3,200 billion. Japan, a far second, held about US$1,100 billion, while the next highest included such emerging countries as Russia, Saudi Arabia, Korea, Taiwan, and other emerging markets. By the end of 2010, public debt as a percentage of GDP for the G7 nations exceeded 95%. That's more than three times the approximately 30% for emerging markets. The total debt-to-GDP ratio including both public and private debt for developed countries such as Japan, the United Kingdom, Portugal, Spain, and the United States exceeded 200%, and in the case of Japan, it was more than 350%. On the other end of the spectrum, the percentages for emerging countries ranged from less than 50% for Russia and less than 80% for Turkey to about 110% for Brazil and India.

It is thus easy to understand why emerging markets are increasingly accepted as satisfying the investment objectives of portfolio diversification and higher returns. This is why investors in the United States, Europe, and Japan are increasingly restructuring their holdings to reduce domestic and developed market exposure in exchange for emerging market exposure. However, this is not being done fast enough. As we have pointed out, emerging stock markets currently account for more than 30% of the world's market capitalization, whereas on average, U.S. institutional investors have only

3 to 8% weightings dedicated to emerging markets. This means that most investors are very underweight emerging markets in their portfolios. So, as more and more investors begin to realize the strong growth potential of emerging markets equities, we expect to see more and more money to go into those markets.

Chapter Three

Discovering Frontier Markets

~

Don't Miss the First Mover Advantage

DURING A RECENT TRIP to Lagos in Nigeria, I got stuck in a hotel elevator not once but twice. I must admit, though, this was not atypical even for the nicest hotels in some emerging market cities. This experience speaks to the demand for more power sources in emerging countries, particularly frontier countries such as Nigeria, since that hotel, like other hotels and businesses in Nigeria, had to depend on its own diesel generators to produce electric power because the public power system was so unreliable, and in this case, the hotel generator failed.

In recent years, it has been widely recognized that among the emerging markets are numerous new markets that are showing even faster growth. These newer emerging markets, which we call "frontier markets," are found all over the world—in Latin America, Africa, Eastern Europe, and Asia. The list is long and includes such countries as Nigeria, Saudi Arabia, Kazakhstan, Bangladesh, Vietnam, United Arab Emirates, Qatar, Egypt, Ukraine, Romania, Argentina, and many more countries that have been underresearched or ignored totally because they were too small or perceived as being too risky or too difficult to enter because of foreign exchange restrictions and other investor barriers.

Why Invest in Frontier Markets?

In the period from 2001 to 2010, the top 10 fastest-growing countries have all been emerging markets but nine of those have been frontier markets. It is surprising to learn that those fastest-growing countries, in addition to China, included the frontier markets of Angola, Myanmar, Nigeria, Ethiopia, Kazakhstan, Chad, Mozambique, Cambodia, and Rwanda. In 2010, Vietnam grew by 6%, Nigeria by 7%, and Qatar by 18.5%, compared to the average of about 2% for developed economies.

Nine of the top 10 fastest-growth countries have been frontier markets.

The future potential growth is also great. Although 16% of the world's land area and 17% of the world's population is in frontier markets, only 6% of the world's gross domestic product is in those markets. That gap is being closed rapidly given their fast growth rates as more and more countries catch up in production and consumption. For example, let's look at the penetration of mobile phone usage in several of these markets. Whereas in 2010, the penetration of mobile phones in Japan and the United States was more than 90%, in Nigeria it was only 55%, and in Bangladesh only 46%. But they are catching up fast as per capita incomes rise and distribution/communications systems expand.

As we have said, these frontier markets are markets that normally investors would shy away from because they may be perceived as being too risky, too small, and too illiquid. However, we have found them to be not only faster growing but also with a number of characteristics that make them safer than imagined. For example, they generally have lower debt and higher foreign exchange reserves in relation to their gross domestic product. With economic growth comes capital market growth, these markets are quickly moving from small and illiquid to large and liquid.

Many of the frontier market countries have enormous reserves of natural resources. Companies that are strong producers of commodities such as oil, iron ore, aluminum, copper, nickel, and platinum look especially interesting. Infrastructure development in emerging markets has led to continued demand for hard commodities, but demand for soft commodities such as sugar, cocoa, and select grains has also increased. Many of the frontier countries are already leading producers of oil, gas, precious metals, and other raw materials and are well positioned to benefit from the growing global demand for these resources.

In the consumer area, the rising per capita incomes mean that the demand for consumer products is increasing fast. The deceleration of population growth combined with high economic growth means that per capita income is rising and demand for consumer products is increasing. This has led to positive earnings growth outlooks for consumer-related companies. We look for opportunities in areas not only related to consumer products, such as automobiles and retailing, but also related to consumer services such as finance, banking, and telecommunications.

Additionally, as the economies of frontier market countries expand, they continue to increase investments in infrastructure, offering interesting opportunities in the construction, transportation, and telecommunications industries. Rising consumption provides these economies with strong purchasing power and the ability to spend their way into growth. Moreover, frontier market countries have been, and continue to be, positively impacted by the substantial investments made by large emerging market countries such as China, India, Russia, and Brazil.

The relatively low correlation of frontier markets to global markets also provides investors with an opportunity to diversify their investment portfolios. Furthermore, the economic drivers across frontier markets are diverse. For example, Botswana, one of the world's largest diamond exporters, is introducing data processing centers. Kazakhstan, a country rich in oil and other natural resources, is making significant investments in infrastructure development. These varied economic themes across frontier markets ensure the opportunity to build a diversified portfolio.

The rising number of initial public offerings (IPOs) in the frontier markets demonstrates that local capital markets have been steadily gaining strength. This is largely a result of governments selling some of their state-owned companies and assets to the public through stock market listings while entrepreneurs have increasingly been using the capital markets as a source of funding for business expansion. The increase in IPOs has, in turn, boosted the overall equity market capitalization of the frontier market universe and is starting to bring these countries and companies to the attention of more investors.

Dig Deeper to Find Gold

Furthermore, frontier markets are generally underresearched. They thus tend to be ignored by the majority of investors. For example, in one month in 2010, approximately 30,000 company research reports were produced in the United States by brokers, banks, and other organizations. In Nigeria, the number was less than 100. This lack of information for investors can be a plus for those willing to do original on-the-spot research. Thus frontier markets display even greater opportunities for those who are willing to do their research, visit the frontier market companies, and dig for information.

The fact that frontier markets are not well known and that not many investors are active in them (yet) means that there are opportunities to be found. Time spent on due diligence to assess the quality of the management team, including more frequent on-site visits to evaluate the business effectively, can uncover great opportunities. A visit is crucial, as examinations of office operations and factories often yield critical insights that cannot be seen through reading financial statements. A meeting with the company's managers or a tour of the company's factories can provide a wealth of knowledge that may otherwise remain undiscovered. Of course, I understand that visiting companies may not be practical for individual investors. This is where the company's annual reports and website as well as the Internet can be very valuable tools. There is a wide spectrum of information available at your fingertips. Dig deeper. Don't just look at the financials of a company; research the people behind the numbers, learn about the industry, and look into competitors—you could learn useful information.

You'll notice that along with visiting individual companies, it's also important to keep your eyes open as soon as you land at a city, and to form a complete picture of the market, the company, and the people. Even small things, like how modern the airport is, the efficiency of public transportation, how crowded a restaurant or hotel might be, and whether there are many tourists, can teach you a lot about the local dynamics and the willingness as well as speed to modernize and compete, which are, eventually, important drivers of stock markets.

Go Ahead, Feel the Excitement

————————— ∼ —————————

**Stay excited about frontier markets because,
in the future, many of them are likely to become
quite important and eventually become
full-fledged emerging markets.**

Stay excited about frontier markets because, in the future, many of them are likely to become quite important and eventually become full-fledged emerging markets. Their potential for economic growth and development remains considerable, especially if the current trend toward the implementation of political and economic reforms remains on course.

Field Note: Kazakhstan

September 2010

Kazakhstan is becoming increasingly important as an investment destination. It has vast natural resources such as oil, gas, copper, uranium, and a host of other minerals. As a result of the billions of dollars pouring into the country to develop those resources, Kazakhstan could become an economic engine for Central Asia. The purpose of my visit was to take a closer look at the mining sector. Prices for several commodities, including metals such as palladium, platinum, copper, gold, and silver, rose dramatically in 2010, and that significantly benefited Kazakh metals and mining companies.

Growing consumerism and wealth were evident in Almaty, Kazakhstan's largest city, as I watched skiers shoot down a mountainside overlooking the city at a new stadium built for the 2011 Asian Games. At a mega-mall, I saw shops you would find in malls all over the world. However, improvement in general living standards still has a way to go.

Here are some notes from my visit:

Mining: My team and I took a one-and-a-half-hour flight to a mining conglomerate's headquarters and its mine site. At one of the firm's four mines in the area, a comprehensive safety briefing was provided by an enthusiastic safety engineer. Dressed in mining clothes with oxygen containers, masks, and hard hats with electric torches, my analysts and I descended 140 meters into the ground in a steel elevator cage. After going

(*Continued*)

through a few iron doors, we boarded a diesel-powered all-terrain vehicle and drove three kilometers through lighted tunnels to the face of one mining site.

After ascending from the mine, my team and I traveled to the concentrating and smelting plants, where the ore is crushed and put in pools of reagents to extract the metal and other minerals. This slurry is then put in circular settling tanks where the concentrate floats to the top and is extracted, dried, smelted into cathodes, and then melted into ingots. I saw piles of gleaming ingots with shipping slips addressed to China. The Chinese influence seems to be strong: The conglomerate is receiving billion of dollars in financing from a Chinese bank, and it has a joint venture with a Chinese firm to develop another mining project.

This trip served us well to understand the important mining sector in Kazakhstan, as well as how efficient the company's mining operations were.

Chapter Four

Getting Down
to Business

~

How to Invest in
Emerging Markets

ONCE YOU'VE DECIDED you will move into emerging markets, the next question to decide for yourself is how to invest. The challenging world of emerging market investments holds great rewards, but also substantial risks for the investor. The criteria to be applied when evaluating the desirability of investments in those markets vary depending on your investment style and objectives.

As an investment manager, I believe in the efficacy of mutual fund investment and will outline why in this chapter. However, some investors may have a preference for purchasing stocks themselves, so I include a review of investment instruments and how to use them.

Primary investment instruments to access emerging markets may be summarized as follows:

- Emerging market mutual funds.
- Domestic listings of emerging market companies.
- Depositary certificate listings of emerging market companies in developed stock markets.
- Exchange-traded funds.

Let's get started by looking at mutual fund investments.

Emerging Market Mutual Funds

Emerging market trusts and funds as we know them today began in 1986, with the launch of an emerging markets fund for institutional investors by Capital International and the International Finance Corporation (IFC). Individual retail investors were able to invest in emerging market funds in 1987, when Templeton launched its New York Stock Exchange–listed Templeton Emerging Markets

Fund, Inc. At that time, no other U.S.-based mutual funds invested significant portions of their portfolios outside the United States. But today more than 27,000 mutual funds globally invest in international securities. And more than 6,000 of those invest exclusively in emerging markets.

Funds make the process of investing much more accessible, and require much less monitoring and research on a day-to-day basis.

Funds make the process of investing much more accessible, and require much less monitoring and research on a day-to-day basis. There are solid reasons for selecting funds as your instrument of investment: gaining exposure to potential high returns and reduced portfolio risk while shielding yourself from the complications of direct equity market purchases.

Closed-End Funds

A closed-end fund (in the United Kingdom they are called investment trusts) operates like any publicly listed company on a stock exchange. The fund raises capital by issuing a fixed number of shares via an initial public offering (IPO). These shares are then listed and traded freely on the market.

At the very early stages of emerging market development, closed-end country funds were a popular way of establishing emerging markets and putting them on the map among investors in the United States, Europe, and Japan. At that time, because of the low liquidity of emerging market stocks, it was felt that a closed-end structure would be best. In an open-end mutual fund structure, investors may redeem their investment from the fund manager at any time; in the closed-end structure, they are not able to ask for their investment back from the fund manager but must realize their investment by selling to other holders. In this way, the fund manager would not be challenged with a situation where many investors suddenly ask to redeem but the manager finds it difficult to sell the portfolio shares. Investment trusts or closed-end funds are sold just like common shares, with the transactions going through stockbrokers, where normal commissions are paid.

Of course, closed-end funds also provide investor a way to gain access and exposure to an emerging market without facing all the problems encountered when entering the markets themselves. In addition, since these country funds were closed-end funds and traded on the major stock exchanges, they were liquid, and investors could enter and exit the market rather simply.

There can be differences in emerging markets funds' performance in view of the wide range of individual market behavior. One significant problem is that during certain periods of time, an emerging markets fund's share price performance may not correspond with the actual value of the portfolio. Each day the net asset value (NAV) of the portfolio is calculated by dividing the total value of all the companies held in the portfolio, including cash and excluding any liabilities, by the number of outstanding fund shares. However, on the stock market where the closed-end fund is listed, the price of each fund share may not correspond to the NAV. Sometimes there may be a premium and sometimes a discount. The range of premiums or discounts can be wide. A discount indicates investor sentiment toward emerging markets is negative and/or they feel that the manager of the fund is not adding value to the fund. A premium, where the fund share price is higher than the NAV, indicates that investors are optimistic about emerging markets and/or believe the fund manager is doing a good job to enhance the NAV of the fund assets.

For buyers of closed-end funds, one of the greatest advantages is that they often sell at attractive discounts to their net asset values. In this way investors may purchase a basket of assets at a discount to their market value. Thus calculating the percentage difference between the share price and the net asset value per share is a key factor. Other factors to be studied are the percentage of total assets held in cash, the geographical spread of the investments, and the historical total return measured in terms of the performance of the NAV per share.

Open-End Funds

It is usually easiest to describe open-end funds as the opposite of closed-end funds. The differences between open-end and closed-end funds are numerous. However, the most important difference is the relationship between price and NAV. As we have said, the NAV of a fund is based on the sum total of all the market values of the fund's securities positions in addition to cash, and less any liabilities. In the case of open-end funds or unit trusts (as they are called in the United Kingdom) the managers must be continuously ready to offer shares to incoming investors at the current NAV plus any sales charges and expenses. They also stand ready to redeem investor shares at NAV less any charges. In contrast, as discussed previously, in the case of closed-end funds, the holder must sell his shares in the market to obtain his money. The important element is that prices of open-end funds are the same as their NAV, whereas the share price of a closed-end fund is determined by the market and tends to differ from the NAV.

Both open-end and closed-end funds offer advantages, the most important of which are:

- Diversification.
- Professional fund management.
- Lower costs as compared to investing individually.
- Convenience in record keeping.

In open-end funds there is a tendency for flows into the fund to increase at the peak of bull markets and outflows to increase in bear markets. This could make it difficult for the fund manager to perform at his or her best. However, if investors cooperate with the fund manager and invest more money when the markets are down, then, in fact, open-end funds could be more advantageous than closed-end funds.

One advantage of closed-end funds or investment trusts is that investors can precisely control the price at which they purchase the shares. In open-end funds, the price at which the shares are purchased is not known until after the investor has made the commitment, since the NAV would be computed at the end of the trading day. Of course, in most cases the differences between the NAV from day to day are normally not great.

Domestic Listings of Emerging Market Companies

For the average investor with limited time, the most difficult method of investing in emerging markets is by directly investing in stocks listed on emerging stock markets. Such direct investments, because of unique local conditions or local investor sentiments, can result in spectacular returns or spectacular losses. When making such direct investments, there are numerous considerations such as foreign currency changes and their impact on the investment as well as the business in which you are investing.

Depositary Certificate Listings of Emerging Market Companies in Developed Stock Markets

For those who prefer to take advantage of foreign stocks without going to a foreign market or foreign currency, depositary receipts such as American depositary receipts (ADRs) and global depositary receipts (GDRs) are designed to give you just that chance.

Depositary receipts are receipts for shares of a foreign company deposited in that foreign country and traded on that foreign stock market. For example, American depositary receipts are traded in the United States. Normally American banks will have a custodial operation in the foreign country where the shares are traded. The shares are kept in the custodian's vault in that foreign country, and then depositary receipts are issued against those shares.

Global depositary receipts are similar instruments, but they are traded in international exchanges, mainly in London and other European markets. They differ from American depositary receipts since they provide issuers with a means of tapping global capital markets by simultaneously issuing one security in multiple markets. Global depositary receipt issues often benefit from better-coordinated global offerings, a broadened shareholder base, and increased liquidity.

The advantage of depositary receipts is that they enable investors in the United States and Europe to invest in an emerging market company without leaving their home market. In some cases, the home market brokerage costs and other costs associated with purchasing and holding shares are even lower than in the emerging market. By not going into the emerging markets directly, the investor avoids considerable administrative and other complications. In addition, dividend collection and distribution are completed much more efficiently since the sponsoring bank undertakes to collect all dividends, and then distributes them to the depositary receipt holders after converting them into U.S. Dollars or the holder's home market currency.

The disadvantages of depositary receipts are that they may sell at a higher price than the underlying stock in the home market, and they are sometimes less liquid than the underlying stocks.

Exchange-Traded Funds

Exchange-traded funds (ETFs) are much like closed-end funds in the sense that they are traded on a stock exchange much like stocks. An ETF has stocks in its portfolios and the manager attempts to hold the total value of assets close to its net asset value over the course of a trading date. Most ETFs have an objective of tracking an index. In the case of emerging market ETFs, they may want to track the MSCI Emerging Markets Index, the S&P/IFCI index, or others.

An ETF thus combines the valuation feature of a open-end fund with the trading feature of a closed-end fund. ETFs were launched in the United States in 1998 and in Europe in 1999 as index funds, but in 2008, the U.S. Securities and Exchange Commission authorized the creation of actively managed ETFs.

ETFs are sometimes attractive because they enable the investor to closely follow an index of stocks and, like closed-end funds, have stock-like features. In volatile markets, it is sometimes difficult for the ETF manager to exactly track a particular index if there is a great deal of volatility.

There is no guarantee that an ETF will always trade at exactly its NAV. If there happens to be strong investor demand, the ETF share price would rise above its NAV per share. This gives an opportunity for speculators to trade on the difference with the knowledge that the ETF manager will need to bring the NAV and price together again.

Managers of ETFs tend to use various arbitrage methods to ensure that the share price tracks the net asset value. Usually the price deviation between the daily closing price and the daily NAV is less than 2%, but sometimes the price deviations may be quite large.

Is There a Right Way to Invest?

Comparing Investment Styles

I CAN STILL RECALL how much grief I received in 1999 from various investment critics when I refused to pay exorbitant prices for technology stocks. The share prices were unreasonable, making valuations extremely expensive and unjustified. There was a clear disconnect between earnings and stock prices. Yes, the funds I managed suffered some short-term underperformance, but over the long term, it paid off when those technology stocks crashed. It pays to look (or in this case, study) before you leap. I must say that I wasn't surprised when the bubble burst in 2000, when investors punished companies that failed to deliver expected profits by dumping their stocks. Investors who withstood the pressure and temptations of investing during those times of "irrational exuberance" were rewarded.

Too much time has been used up over the years by trying to determine which investment style is the most successful. All kinds of terminology have sprung up to describe the strategies employed: "technical," "fundamental," "active," "passive," "bottom-up," "top-down," "value," and "growth." Instead of rehashing the debate, I'll outline my personal investment approach and explain why I think it makes sense for any equity investor.

Value versus Growth Orientation

Sir John Templeton once said that there was a tendency for too many investors to focus on "outlook" or "trend." It was his belief that more opportunities could be uncovered by focusing on value and I agree with that.

Studies have shown that over the long term, stock market prices tend to be influenced by the asset value and earnings capabilities of listed shares. Also, share prices tend to fluctuate much more widely than real share values.

———————— ∿ ————————

Opportunities can be uncovered by focusing on value.

The value approach to investing was first and best defined by Benjamin Graham and David Dodd in their 1934 book *Security Analysis*. In that book, they articulated the system of buying value shares whose price was cheap relative to factors such as earnings, dividends, or book assets. But studies have also revealed elaborations on the application of that fundamental value orientation. For example, one study showed that investing in shares with a low ratio of share price to cash flow was a better strategy than buying shares with a low ratio of share price to book value. Others indicate that price-to-earnings (P/E) ratios were the best determinant of future price. Needless to say, despite what individual value criteria are used, those indicators that give investors insight into the earnings power and assets of a company are the best paths to finding value.

Many investors speak of "value investing" but few actually diligently apply the value investing principles and perform the hard work necessary to find real value. Those investors who do work hard at it are inevitably rewarded. The investor who purchases a stock that is selling below its intrinsic value can enjoy a certain peace of mind. If, after purchasing a stock at a low price in relation to value, the price continues to decline, then it is simply a better bargain than it was before. A number of studies have shown that dividend-paying companies perform better.

On the flip side, growth investors generally believe in buying stocks with above-average earnings growth without great regard for whether the stock is a bargain. In general, growth investors are more willing to pay a premium for such companies because they expect them to continue growing at such high rates. As a result of their high growth, such companies tend to have higher price-to-earnings and price-to-book value ratios than value stocks. In addition, growth companies tend to have low or even no dividend payouts, as profits tend to be invested into the company to further boost earnings. The main risk here is that the expected growth and profits may not occur. After all, just look back to 1999 when the technology sector was booming and investors were picking up stocks at astronomical prices with little regard for their current value but counting on their high growth to yield good value at a future date. However, when those companies failed to meet the high expectations placed on them, investors dumped their shares faster than you could say "technology crash," which led to the bursting of the 2000 technology bubble.

Historically, growth and value investment styles often do not move in tandem. While the growth market was strong in 1999, investors ignored the benefits of value investing. However, after the technology crash in 2000, the market shifted and value investing began showing signs of strength and dominance. Understanding how an investment is likely to perform under different market conditions can help you avoid selling a fund or stock because its style is temporarily out of favor.

You may now be wondering which strategy is for you or which one makes more sense. I strongly believe that value investing is no doubt the way to go, especially for investors with a long-term horizon in mind. And here's why.

History has taught us that when we buy value stocks, which are trading at low valuations despite strong fundamentals, over time the market will uncover the bargain and yield higher returns. In general, value investors tend to avoid paying unreasonable prices for stocks. However, growth investors tend to pay more attention to high market expectations and are more willing to pay higher and sometimes unreasonable current prices. (Here I must emphasize "current" since a price may seem high now but with high earnings growth that price may appear very cheap in the future.) In cases where expectations fail, value investors have less to lose as the stock has already been trading at low prices. However, in the case of the growth investor, the stock price would plummet and result in heavy losses, as seen with the technology sector in 2000. As a result, growth investing tends to involve greater risk than value investing.

I've been writing this as if there is a clear differentiation between value and growth. The reality is that you as an investor must always be looking to the future, and even when you are seeking value based on current earnings and current prices, you must always have your eye on the future since you expect a value company to at least do as well as it has done in the past and, hopefully, even better. You don't want to buy companies that are not growing, even if they look cheap at current valuations.

Short versus Long Term

Another issue about which I have been particularly concerned is that of evaluation or measurement of returns. Over the years, I have consistently emphasized a long-term investment approach. I have had to write many letters to individual investors in funds I manage who have expressed concern when we have not taken opportunistic short-term positions. Another way observers forget or ignore the long-term approach is obvious when they ask questions like: "Why have the funds experienced a poor performance over the past six months?" I must continually remind investors and commentators that this is the wrong question, and that there is no "poor" six-month performance because sometimes it is necessary to underperform in the short term to outperform in the long term. If you are buying cheap stocks, they are cheap because they are unpopular and they could remain unpopular or even become more unpopular in the short term before the market wakes up and realizes that the stock is undervalued.

One problem facing the world today is the tendency for people to think in shorter and shorter time frames. A study undertaken in the 1990s indicated that stocks in U.S. companies were held for an average of two years, whereas in the 1960s they used to be held for seven years. Some shareholders look for a quick return on their investments, and thus business executives are increasingly driven by the same mentality. This short-term philosophy is detrimental to the health of the company and the investor. Unless companies and investors take a longer-term view, growth prospects are limited and planning becomes stunted. Taking a long view of emerging markets will yield excellent results for the investor prepared to be patient and willing to apply sound and tested principles in a diligent and consistent manner.

The approach we take is not that of a three-month, six-month, or even one-year period, but at least a five-year period. Over the many years that Templeton funds

--- ~ ---

Taking a long view of emerging markets will yield excellent results for the investor prepared to be patient and willing to apply sound and tested principles in a diligent and consistent manner.

---

have been investing, I have found that striving for short-term performance increases the risks to shareholders and actually results in poorer returns. Only by taking the long view will investment managers be able to do the best job for investors.

Bottom-Up versus Top-Down Investment Strategies

There is continuing controversy over the optimal research approach strategy to apply to emerging markets portfolio management, or for that matter any equity portfolio. On one side of the fence is the bottom-up investment school of thought, and on the other side are the top-down investors. Let me make clear from the outset that I think the arcane debate over the merits of narrowly defined investment strategies is often not very productive. Any good fund manager applies all the investment information he or she can obtain to make a good decision, and is unlikely to satisfy pure patterns that are merely convenient definitions.

**Both "bottom-up" and "top-down" research
have a place in successful investing.**

When beginning our investment research we tend to take a "bottom up" approach by studying individual companies wherever they may be located in the world and in whatever industry they may be in. In this sense, the "bottom-up" research focuses on the details of each and every company: What the nature of their business is, how profitable they are, what the value of their assets is, and so on. The "top-down," or macroeconomic and political information, is then used to place the "bottom-up" information in context. No company can exist in isolation, and the economic and political conditions of the country or countries in which it operates will impact profitability and long-term planning. We need to be concerned with macroeconomic and political conditions to the extent that they may hinder or help a bargain company achieve its objectives. Bottom-up investors allow country and sector allocations of their portfolios be determined by bottom-up stock selection while taking into consideration the wider picture.

If an investor wants to take a strictly top-down approach, he or she will first select the countries in which he or she would like to invest, through the analysis of the economic and political environment in those countries. He or she may also study industry sector characteristics to determine which sectors are best. Only after those studies will he or she begin to select individual stocks within those markets and sectors finally looking at value as well as such considerations as liquidity and market capitalization, factors that would influence the manager's ability to enter and exit the market easily. Of course these categorizations of bottom-up and top-down investment styles are gross oversimplifications, and it is difficult to find managers who neatly fit those descriptions. The subject is fraught with dangers, simply because definitions of investment styles tend to pigeonhole particular managers and leave them with fewer options. More often than not, some managers would tend to emphasize stock selection whereas others would tend to emphasize country allocation, but both would at all times be considering macroeconomic and political situations as well as individual stock differences. It is difficult for any manager to ignore matters regarding earnings, growth, and dividends that are inherent in the evaluation of companies while ignoring such macro factors as exchange rates, interest rates, currencies, and other such factors and their impact.

Chapter Six

Researching
Emerging Markets

~

Always Keep an Open Mind

IN EMERGING MARKETS, I am continually reminded of the need for independent research and careful checking of what company managers, brokers, and researchers tell me. You must also constantly be aware not only of the influences and biases that impact their thinking but also those influences and biases affecting you. These influences and biases are strongest in the places where one spends the most time and from where we obtain the most information.

For this reason, it is important to keep an open mind and read news and research reports originating from all over the world and from different sources. You must try your best to exercise a great deal of objectivity in your analysis of all the relevant data, so that local or foreign, company-specific, country-specific, or industry-specific data may be given appropriate weighting.

~

"A verbal promise isn't worth the paper it's written on."

—*Samuel Goldwyn*

There must be an ability and a willingness for the emerging markets investor to obtain information from all relevant sources, whether they're local or international sources. In other words, total reliance cannot be placed on just local information or on only foreign information.

The four best sources of information for emerging markets investors are:

1. The staff of a company in which you are considering an investment.
2. The staff of the company's competitors.

3. The audited financial statements.
4. The company's customers.

Original information is the best. If you read about it in the newspaper or a magazine, then it is probably too late (except maybe to do exactly the opposite of what the article suggests!).

In today's markets, it is has become increasingly difficult, if not impossible, to obtain qualitative and truly independent external advice and opinions. The interest of market participants and advisors have become very entangled and complex, and sometimes corrupted. We need to question the real independence of research conducted by investment banks, as oftentimes, as the past has shown, research of these institutions cannot be entirely independent from the banks' own trading interests and advisory mandates. The many scandals that came to light during the recent financial crisis have proven that point once again.

Market information has to be taken with huge care and there is no substitute for your own hard work in researching and understanding complex situations. Glossy reports have to be handled with care, and the fact alone that there is such a large bias for "buy" or "strong buy" recommendations out there has to trigger alarm bells for the diligent investor. Furthermore, if the broker is distributing the glossy publication to hundreds of investors, then there is little chance of the company still being a bargain by the time you read about it. Therefore, these research reports can be used only for background information.

For the same reason, it is not wise to unquestioningly accept financial data such as financial ratios from external sources, as they might be using a methodology or making adjustments that skew the data to a large degree. Every country has its own ways and definitions—is accustomed to different calculation methodologies—so one has to again be careful when making comparisons.

Reading periodicals and talking with brokers can be useful, but it's best to use more time to try to get to know the company's staff and its competitors. Always use the company's audited financial statements as the primary information source. If you find what seems to be a particularly good independent and reliable information source, use it but make sure it really is reliable.

Obtaining data from advisers and analysts based in the country in which the investments are being made is also beneficial even though it could be biased. As the number of investors and the amount of capital moving into emerging markets escalate, locally obtained knowledge could allow you to find yet undiscovered gems.

Experience has shown me that total reliance on a locally based analyst or adviser is not sufficient. For wise portfolio decisions, two important perspectives are necessary: first, the global outlook and experience that come from having invested in many countries, and second, a more detailed and intimate knowledge that comes from a local presence, especially about individual companies.

It is important to incorporate both perspectives by having local and country-specific information collated, digested, and then contrasted to global data. This analytic process yields much more powerful results than research that leans heavily on one or the other source of information. Locally gathered information, for example, provides insights into the real success of a business, as measured against similar companies in the same country experiencing the same economic conditions. Global information helps you to see what international economic or political forces are gathering steam and may alter the local business environment. The end results are much more valuable insights, which must yield far better long-term investment returns.

All Walks of Life

As an alternative to formal information sources, when visiting the countries in which I invest I like to talk to working people and people who are actually functioning in the economy. The people I have met have told me about their lives and how the economic conditions are affecting them. Take for instance, in 1995, when visiting Brazil, I found that there was a subdued feeling in the country stemming from the economic slowdown. Inflation was down substantially, but the economy itself had also been slowed. As a result, the business leaders I met with were not optimistic. From their perspective alone, I would have developed a rather downbeat economic forecast for the country.

Talking to people on the street, however, changed the picture for me. One woman said, "For the first time in many years I now know how much money I am going to make at the end of the month. In the past, we had 2,000% inflation a year, so each month I didn't know how much I was going to get paid, due to the indexation system for salaries. I had to rush to the bank and get in line to cash the check and then rush to the supermarket to buy anything I could get. Now that inflation is down to 8%, I can plan and I know how much I am going to receive and what it will buy. Of course things are expensive, and I must be careful with my expenditures, but I think things are a lot better." From statements like this, I formed much more accurate expectations of coming consumer attitudes and spending than I did from talking to the businesspeople themselves.

In addition to depending on a lot of respondents from different walks of life, it is important also to use your own associates as sounding boards and sources of information.

One of the key aspects of investing in emerging markets is the need to perform a careful historical analysis of companies. Such historical information requires in-depth research of the company's balance sheet, profit and loss figures, and other financial information going back at least five years, paying particular attention to the potential for, and the stability of, earnings growth. Normally, the further back in time the analysis goes, the better it will be.

Narrowing the Choices

There are tens of thousands of emerging market companies in which you can invest. To narrow these down to a more manageable number, you can use key financial information and ratios such as market capitalization and turnover as well as price-to-earnings, price-to-book, and debt-to-equity ratios.

Factors such as a sound balance sheet, high return on equity, decent sales growth, and good profit margins are some of the items you should look at when you undertake your analysis. Of course for this sort of analysis you need to have reliable and timely access to audited accounts, which can present problems when each country has different accounting standards. Remember, improperly or falsely presented materials can make the difference between buying and avoiding a stock.

Attention to detail is important. Henry Ford once said, "A handful of men have become very rich by paying attention to details that most others ignored." Audited accounts are necessarily the starting place for the examination of any company in the emerging markets. Audited financial statements provide the first source of information an investor has about a particular company. These statements are supposed to show an unbiased account of the company's health and business.

One of the most critical factors in judging any company, telecom, utility, industrial, or what-have-you is the quality of management. So one of the first things I look for, not surprisingly, is any sign of shady dealings or ethical misconduct. If I find or learn of even a hint or wisp of impropriety, I stop there and no longer consider the company viable for investment. Usually, local people know the rumors and can give you insights into behavior that would not be included in any research reports or other publications. By having our own team members based in most markets we invest in, we get a good insight into local dynamics and rumors, scandals, and suspicious developments. Always inquire about the probity and honesty of management before anything else. (I've learned that one the hard way.)

———————————— ≈ ————————————

Always inquire about the probity and honesty of management before anything else.

Number two on my personal checklist are the skills and imagination of management. The best way to check out the management is, as I have said, to meet with the managers personally. But if you can't do that, the next best thing is their annual report, the company's website, and Internet searches. There is a wide range of information freely available on the Internet. You can also sometimes write to the investor relations person at the company if you have any questions on the basis of reading the annual report.

My frequent visits permit me to develop a personal sense of where the company is going and how management maintains the facilities and its employees. The appearance of the staff, operating environment, and physical location can all speak volumes about a company's success and priorities. Meeting with corporate representatives also helps to develop an understanding of the company, giving us more sources of information than the annual company report.

Is It a Buy or a Sell?

We use the time-tested strategy of identifying securities that stand at a low price in relation to the company's long-term value. We also evaluate how a company compares to its local, regional, and industry peers. We study quantitative as well as qualitative factors and five years of historical performance (or as many years back as we can go) and five years of projections. This is usually followed by a company visit and, if everything checks out and the price is below what we consider its fair value, we purchase the shares for the funds that we manage.

For a stock to be included in the funds I manage, it must meet at least two of the following four requirements:

1. It must be cheap relative to its price history, other stocks in the market, or other stocks in its industry internationally.

2. It must have good growth prospects, with a growth rate in excess of inflation projected for the next five years.

3. It must be cheap in relation to its net tangible assets.

4. It demonstrates a concern for minority investors by paying dividends.

Whenever you can buy a large amount of future earnings power for a low price, you have made a good investment. But you must remember to keep your estimates up-to-date with frequent reviews.

When the market price for a particular stock rises above the intrinsic value to an unreasonable extent, the stock can be sold if you can find a stock that is cheaper. Conversely, when the market price falls below the intrinsic value for a particular stock to an unreasonable extent, that stock can be placed on a list of stocks that can be purchased. I liked it when one of my colleagues compared the process to a ladder—when one stock reaches the top, it gets knocked off, and a new one is added to the bottom rung to replace it.

What's Its Worth?

The appraisal of value is complex and subject to numerous uncertainties. Some of these factors are management ability, growth trends, government control, assets per share, average past market prices for the shares, dividends, current earnings, average earnings in previous years, and estimates of future earnings.

With regard to the demands on your analytical skills in evaluating emerging market companies, most daunting are not only the varying accounting standards used in each country but the varying taxation regimes that affect how accounting standards are applied and as a result how accounting items are treated. It is essential, therefore, to ensure that you understand what methods the company's management and accountants are using. Accounting and taxation policies are also not static, so it is important to be aware of changes.

After decades of investing in emerging market companies, I've learned to not only examine profit and loss (P&L) statements and balance sheets, but also to study such issues as market share and technological improvements. But by far the most important single consideration in judging whether a company is over- or undervalued in the marketplace is its ability to grow earnings. A growth in earnings can materialize more easily if the assets that produce the products or services are undervalued and managed by competent people. When you're buying stock in a company, what are you really buying? All sorts of intangibles, to be sure, like goodwill, management skill, a brand name, and the rest. But at the end of the day, what you're really buying is hard assets. Assets, of course, don't always have to be *things*. They can even be receivables—money owed to the company. But whatever those assets are, it's important to know what they are, because the easiest way to determine the legitimate value of a share of stock is to take the value of all those assets and divide them by the number of shares outstanding. That combined with good management can result in a winning company.

∼

If the net asset value (NAV) divided by the number of shares gives you a dollar figure higher than the share price and the company has competent managers, then you could consider it an undervalued stock.

In attempting to determine the NAV of a company, it is necessary to first look to the accountants hired by the company who produce the figures we work with. We use those accounts to make extrapolations of the value of these assets in comparison to other companies around the world.

It should also be remembered that different yardsticks are more significant for some companies than for others. In most cases, the single greatest yardstick is how high the price is in relation to earnings; but of course it is more important to compare price not with present earnings, but with future anticipated earnings. For example, when investigating telecom companies we use a factor such as income per telephone line or income per subscriber as one of a number of means of judging the overall efficiency of the system. In the banking sector, nonperforming loans would be an important indicator, while price to net premiums would be a useful yardstick to compare insurance companies.

When analyzing accounts, keep an eye on the following areas:

- In manufacturing and sales organizations, monitor inventory, accounts receivables, and order backlog trends. These are the strongest indicators of problems and are much more closely related to stock returns than reported earnings.
- Profit margin trends are important.
- There are many ways to appraise financial statements, but one of the most common is the use of ratio analysis, whereby the various elements in financial statements are compared. When looking at the value of a firm, ratios such as price to earnings, dividend yield, return on equity, and price to book value are used. When assessing profitability, ratios such as profit margins, return on equity, and return on assets are used. When assessing safety or balance sheet strength, ratios such as debt to equity and the current ratio can be meaningful indicators.

The bottom line is that all information is useful; none should be ignored, but none should be the sole platform upon which to base an investment decision. Whether your company information is derived from local or global sources, wherever it comes from—brokers, the media, business executives, the people in the street, your associates—consider it all, and then make the most informed decision possible. Only after having lined up all of this company information do we reintroduce macroeconomic factors to see if they are favorable in relation to the company's targets. If yes, then it's a *buy*!

Field Note: Czech Republic

November 2011

During 2011 with all the emphasis on Western Europe's debt problems in the so-called "PIIGS" countries (Portugal, Italy, Ireland, Greece, and Spain), Eastern Europe and Russia were pretty much overlooked.

Of course, that is not to say that a number of countries in Eastern Europe did not have debt problems of their own in the past. Five years

(Continued)

before in Hungary, for example, banks made the mistake of offering mortgage loans in Swiss Francs and Japanese Yen because interest rates in those currencies were so much lower than those for the Hungarian Forint and thus were attractive to their clients.

However, when the Hungarian Forint went from 141 to the Swiss Franc in July 2008 to 253 by November 2011, a devaluation of 79%, many Hungarian mortgage holders got into trouble.

During my meetings in Prague, however, I found that businesses my team and I visited remained relatively unscathed by the issues in other parts of Europe. Companies visited included:

Banking: Operating in a healthy economy, the Prague banks were in fairly good shape. I was satisfied with the balance sheet of one of the banks I visited and was happy to hear that it was considering dividend payouts. Some difficulties were, however, expected in the Eurozone due to its importance as an export destination for the Czech Republic as well as an increase in value-added tax (VAT).

Electric Utilities: The largest Czech power company had significant nuclear and coal-fired generation capacities that made it one of the most profitable electricity players in the region. The power company has also taken advantage of the single, liberalized European market, where there were no barriers in exporting or importing electricity to and from neighboring countries, especially Germany. As a result, prices in the Czech Republic were able to rise up to the level charged by their counterparts in Western Europe thus benefiting the Czech producer.

Gaming: One interesting meeting was with a leading fixed-odds betting operator with an extensive branch network in Central and Eastern Europe. The management was of the opinion that gambling was a recession-resistant business since people would still gamble in tough times—similarly to drinking and smoking, I presume. The company also voiced its interest in acquisitions, possibly in Greece.

All in all, on this trip I found that things were quite normal in some Prague companies despite all the gloomy news floating around about Europe.

Chapter Seven

The Reality of Risk

~

And Why Not to Fear It

MODERN PORTFOLIO THEORY GIVES a technical definition of "risk" that is very different from what we would normally think of risk. It defines risk as volatility calculated by the variance (as measured by the correlation coefficient) of a portfolio's historical returns. Therefore, a portfolio that is yielding excellent returns to an investor may have a "high-risk" profile if those returns have been volatile over the years.

Investing in emerging markets is not, they say, for the faint of heart. But then again, as the U.S. subprime crisis showed us, neither is investing in developed markets.

Any progress requires risk, since progress is made by moving into the unknown or the unexpected, with the possibility of making mistakes. To make progress we must be able to adapt and diversify so that any one mistake will not destroy our entire portfolio.

If we've learned anything in the past few years, it's that emerging markets are not as risky, in the traditional sense, as they were 10 or 20 years ago. If anything, some of the more mature emerging markets could be said to be even safer than the so-called developed markets, since the growth prospects are so much better. This clearly seems to be the case when you compare emerging market giants such as China and Brazil with developed economies such as Italy and Spain. However, risk in the sense of volatility still exists and because of high velocity trading, derivatives, and more efficient global trading networks, that volatility has actually increased in not only emerging markets but also in developed markets.

One solution to minimize portfolio volatility and thereby the risk (i.e., making your returns as close to constant as possible) is to invest in countries with markets that have a low relation or correlation with each other. By investing in stocks of countries that have low correlation coefficients with each other, the volatility of your global portfolio is reduced, and, by extension, the risk to your investment.

Of course, the volatility definition of risk and the relatively simple solution for reducing volatility through diversification does not explain the entire picture of risk in emerging markets investments.

The Big Picture

Over the years, I've become all too familiar with the significant risks that investors face in emerging markets. In no particular order, they include:

- *Political risk:* The possibility that revolutions or political turmoil in a country could significantly impact the value of an investment.
- *Currency risk:* The impact on an investment of fluctuations in a national currency.
- *Company risk:* Any risk arising from exposure to a particular company, such as the lack of information, a change in the company's management or

ownership, a change in the health of a business, depression in a particular industrial sector, or a sudden price panic.

- *Broker risk:* Risk of unscrupulous or dishonest brokers who use customer orders to "front run," that is, to buy or sell ahead of their clients to take advantage of the market price differences.

- *Settlement risk:* Problems experienced in trying to settle transactions, and in obtaining, registering, and paying for securities.

- *Custodial risk:* Exposure to local safekeeping agents (popularly known as custodians) who may not provide adequate security for clients' shares.

- *Operational risk:* Risk arising from inadequate auditing and bookkeeping standards.

- *Market risk:* Exposure to extreme fluctuations in market values and the lack of liquidity.

I've disclosed all the major risks I can think of. So why, you might well ask after reviewing that list, should anyone bother with these messy, risky, strange situations? Because those risks exist in all markets, emerging and developed, and diversification internationally reduces the impact of such risks.

If you want to hit the financial home runs of the future, you'll need to pay attention to what goes on not only in your home country but everywhere in the world. In 2011, emerging market companies accounted for over 30% of the world's market capitalization, according to the World Federation of Exchanges. Thus, even the most prudent investors in search of diversification and asset allocation should consider investing one-third of their total portfolios in emerging markets, whether that investment be made in individual stocks or in an ever-growing list of emerging markets mutual funds.

As I have pointed out, historical stock market performances in emerging markets also back up the view that emerging markets have outperformed developed markets.

Before deciding to invest in any region, country, or company, all possible risks must be considered and one of the first to examine is the market liquidity, the investor's ability to buy and sell a stock quickly and efficiently. If a market or stock turnover is low, of course the ability to buy or sell is hindered, which is a disadvantage. However, in illiquid markets the difference between the buy and sell prices or the "spread" can be wide, thus opening up an opportunity to purchase at bargain prices. Therefore, investing in a low-liquidity, low-activity market can generate phenomenal returns because the purchase of just a few stocks by a few investors can drive the prices of those shares up dramatically. Of course, following the same pattern, a major sell-off in an illiquid market can cause prices to drop catastrophically.

Journalist Christopher Fildes once noted: "An emerging market is a market from which you cannot emerge in an emergency!" This is true of illiquid markets, but such markets should not be ignored since they could contain some excellent investments.

If there is anything we've learned in the past few years, it is that developed markets can be as volatile as emerging ones. During crisis times, it isn't uncommon to see a 5% swing in some markets in one day. But don't fly off to the United States for a safer ride: The stock market there also had its fair share of ups and downs, as was evident during the subprime crisis.

How to avoid being sideswiped by these risks?

Hedging Your Bets

Let's take another look at that map of the world. If you could overlay a transparent sheet with a graph of market lows and highs over time, you would see that with few exceptions, regional boundaries still very much define emerging markets.

In an age when jet travel and electronic commerce would seem to dominate an increasingly global economy, it's surprising how strong local and regional boundaries are. Regional economies in the less industrialized, less wired parts of the world are obviously knit together by increasingly advanced communications and transportation links. Therefore, changes in one country can impact an entire region.

For better or for worse, when the Mexico Peso crisis hit in 1994, the entire Latin American region suffered from what global investors quickly dubbed the tequila effect. In the same vein, when international currency traders began to seize on weaknesses in the Association of South East Asian Nations (ASEAN) countries—Indonesia, Malaysia, and Thailand primarily—the ripple effect that coursed through the region was called the Asian currency contagion and the Asian financial flu.

In both regions, certain countries (Hong Kong in Asia, Chile in Latin America) stood to some degree above the fray. But all global investors contemplating where to put whatever funds are at their disposal should first ponder the impact of regional changes and input that information in their research calculations. It is important to remember, however, that these regional movements where all countries in one region move together in one direction are temporary, and after a crisis, each country—each company—adopts its own behavior and stock price changes, which can be highly uncorrelated.

So, what should you do when there is a market crisis and it seems that all the stock markets are on fire?

Sit Tight, Don't Worry, Be Happy

If you have done your homework and selected a well managed mutual fund or put together a well diversified portfolio of undervalued stocks, then the best thing to do is: "Sit tight, don't worry, be happy." As long as the fundamentals are on the money, the companies will bounce back again, usually stronger than ever before. Please remember: Your best protection is diversification and patience is more than its own (just) reward.

If someone tells me he wants to become rich in less than one year in emerging markets, I tell him to take his money elsewhere. The swings in stock markets make market timing difficult and, if your timing is terrible, it can be very costly. The only way to consistently stay ahead of the game is to adopt a long-term view and, if appropriate, with a strong contrarian spin.

When we look at the balance sheet of a company, we might be willing to pay a high P/E ratio if we think that the company will achieve the high growth needed to obtain what might become a low P/E ratio in five years' time.

The single most important lesson I've learned is that long-term planning pays. The reason for this is astoundingly simple. All markets are fundamentally cyclical. Like people—because they're composed of the aggregate decisions people make—they're given to extended bouts of irrational fear and panic and equally irrational exuberance.

The single most important lesson I've learned is that long-term planning pays.

Like adolescents, we can get a little bit carried away at times. But—and I can't repeat this enough—it is by riding these wild mood swings like a surfer taking a wave that the investor can make money. An entirely rational market, after all, is a market that would barely budge at all.

The time of maximum pessimism is the best time to buy, and the time of maximum optimism is the best time to sell. That seems counterintuitive, right? Well, it is, and therefore it requires a positively stoic ability to let your mind rule over your passions. This brings us unerringly to: If you can see the light at the end of the tunnel, it's probably too late to buy (or sell).

Chapter Eight

Timing Market Factors: Currencies

Why a Crisis Can Be the Best Time to Buy

― ❦ ―

MARKET TIMING, ON A consistent basis, successfully, is impossible. However there are conditions when it is the best time to buy and the best time to sell. The guide to such conditions can be found in company valuations. But those valuations are impacted by currency changes. Contagion from the financial crisis that swept through the Asian markets like wildfire helped to strike panic in the hearts of even the most stalwart and savvy investors. On the face of it, that's not too hard to understand. After all, when a foreign currency declines in value, any stock that you own denominated in that currency is going to decline in value relative to the strength of one of the global reserve currencies, such as the U.S. Dollar, unless there is a local currency price increase that compensates for the local currency's devaluation.

So what to do during a currency crisis? Well, the first thing to realize is that despite everyone ranting about destitution and impoverishment, a devalued currency is not necessarily a catastrophe for any economy. In fact, it can be the engine for the next cycle of growth. There are winners and losers in such conditions. A cheap currency can mean that exporters will find it easier to export their goods, while importers will have difficulty.

Understanding Foreign Exchange

When examining foreign exchange (forex) and the expected value of a currency relative to other currencies, it is important to understand not only how forex traders behave but also some fundamentals. One of the most important is called the purchasing power parity (PPP). This is a way of comparing inflation in one country to inflation in another country. If inflation in Country A is higher than inflation in Country B, then it would be expected that Country A's currency will get weaker than Country B's. It's best to construct a line chart showing the trend of this relationship by dividing the monthly inflation rate in, say, the United States by the inflation rate in, say, Thailand. If inflation in Thailand is higher than in the United States and we track the monthly PPP line over time, the moving line will help us project if the currency is over- or undervalued and if the Thai Baht is expected to weaken or strengthen against the U.S. Dollar, as illustrated in the accompanying chart.

Purchasing Power Parity Chart of the Thai Baht

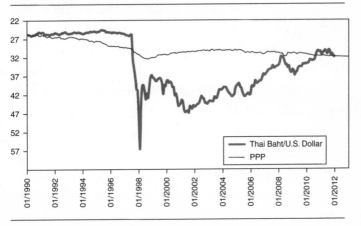

You can tell at a glance whether a particular currency is strengthening or weakening against the U.S. Dollar, which helps keep currency risk in perspective. The reason that the PPP index works so well to determine the strength or weakness of a given currency is that one of the key indicators of weakness in any economy is, of course, inflation.

Despite the bad rap that currency speculators—they prefer to be called forex traders—get in the press, a wise global investor will always do well to try to think like a foreign exchange trader, if for no better reason than to anticipate their next moves.

Global currency traders spend a great deal of time probing for weaknesses in a nation's defenses. High inflation rates are a big sign of weakness, and a form of bait to the wily forex trader.

The second thing that forex traders tend to look at is current account balances or imbalances. A country's current account factors in all of its imports, exports, payments out, and payments in. A high current account deficit could raise concerns. Some countries take into consideration so-called invisibles, as opposed to just hard trade numbers, to correctly assess, for example, the value of services as opposed to simply trade in hard goods.

The Upside of Political Uncertainty

The third thing forex traders look at is the political environment. If something looks odd to them on the political side, they'll dump a currency without remorse. In one country we found an extremely unpopular prime minister who only made matters worse by delaying and showing uncertainty in the face of a rapidly devaluing currency when decisive and fast decisions were needed.

In retrospect, it wasn't so hard to figure out why he and his cabinet were all so unconcerned in the face of a currency disaster: Personally, most of them were worth billions, not millions. And that's not in their local currency but in U.S. greenbacks. This military man turned politician failed to purge shady power brokers from his cabinet, and couldn't keep from meddling in the positive policies of the few brave-hearted bureaucrats truly committed to financial reform. In short, this guy was a walking disaster, and the very personification of a major risk of global investing: political risk. However, once the crisis hit, the Thai people

---

Political uncertainty—like any other form of uncertainty—can be your green light to move into a market.

---

got out a big broom and swept these guys out of power, which is one of the reasons these periodic crises are not such a bad thing: They promote much-needed change.

Overcoming Your Fears and Moving On

Uncertainty depresses stock prices. If you have faith in your own analysis and research—an uncertain atmosphere can be just the break that you've been looking for to pick up wonderful, inexpensive stocks that otherwise would be too expensive to even consider.

When many markets are crashing, what do you do? Where do you go? Is there nowhere to run? Nowhere to hide? Does it make sense to race for the exits? In a word: No.

What I try to do is not behave like a sheep but behave like a shark. The great thing about market crashes is that now all of a sudden, all sorts of stocks we had been look-ing at but rejecting as too expensive were now affordable, for the first time in years.

At one particularly dire point in one of the market crises, one stock market had fallen by over 70% from its peak! Why? You know perfectly well why. Because all the smart money was groaning that it would take at least five years for recovery to take place. Of course, that was not the case and within one year, the market shot up to its previous high and instead of rushing for the exits everyone was rushing to the enter the market. There are many such cases we can point to. After the Mexican tequila crisis in 1996, it took only two years for the Mexican market to bounce back.

Often market commentators tend to try to draw parallels between one crisis and another, but each one is different and it is dangerous to make quick judgments since each country, each company, and each sector is different, and most should be individually considered based on their own merits. For example, in early 2012, many commentators were predicting a crash in the Chinese property market with dire consequences for banks and the economy as a whole. Unfortunately they were looking at the Chinese property market through the lens of the subprime property crisis in the United States. Such a comparison was faulty because the economic conditions and structure of both markets are markedly different. Looking at just one variable, derivatives, the U.S. property market was heavily influenced by credit default swaps (CDSs), which had no influence on the Chinese property market.

In deciding whether to buy given stocks, one local analyst observed that most investors and even many analysts and brokers were often acting more on raw emotion than anything else. As a result, the real talent is not necessarily the ability to identify good companies, but the ability to anticipate which stock the masses of overly emotional investors will rush to next—making sure that you are ready and aware of these mood changes.

Don't forget that reading local papers and watching local newscasts can provide valuable insights unavailable anywhere else into the mentality of local markets.

The amount of unreliable predictions about the Mexican meltdown of 1994 and the tequila effect that spoiled Latin American markets for a few years was remarkable. But even more remarkable—though much less remarked upon—is the salient fact that you never, ever saw a front-page headline that blared: "Mexican Markets Stage Fast Recovery."

The problem with recoveries is that they don't make good copy. Market meltdowns make headlines. Market recoveries make money.

$\sim$

Market meltdowns make headlines. Market recoveries make money.

The thing that I find interesting about market commentators is that, much like those they seek to advise, they tend to go to extremes: "It's a disaster!" "It's a catastrophe!" "There's blood in the streets!" Now, if you can, take away all those exclamation points from all those opinions. Don't you feel better? More calm? More collected?

Okay, take a deep breath, count to 10—and start thinking about going on a shopping spree. A classic quote often attributed to the first Baron Rothschild is that the best time to buy is when there's "blood in the streets." The second part of that bit of advice, I was told, is "even when the blood is your own." This obviously makes the Baron even more interesting than I thought he was.

I would personally amend that to take the subjective factor into account: The best time to buy is when everyone else is screaming that there's blood in the streets. Because I'm willing to bet that no matter what happens, if you take a look down into that gutter, all you're likely to see is a gutter full of wine.

Field Note: South Korea

August 2011

The South Korean economy and stock market had been doing fairly well in recent years. Although the GDP growth fell because of the subprime crisis, there was a dramatic recovery in 2010. Like other

(Continued)

emerging market currencies, the Korean Won was steadily strengthening against the U.S. Dollar.

My meetings in Seoul reflected the changing business environment in South Korea with a move into higher-value-added products and advanced technology.

Home shopping was also on the rise in South Korea, and the field was getting crowded with many newcomers. As a result, competition for popular cable TV channels was heating up among home shopping companies as well as new multichannel providers.

Other strong industries in South Korea include:

Shipbuilding: South Korea had one of the world's leading shipbuilding industries. Large shipbuilders had been benefiting from the boom in offshore oil drilling production rigs as well as sophisticated liquid natural gas carriers.

Construction: In addition to shipbuilders, South Korean construction and engineering firms were active globally. One major firm we met had a diversified business portfolio ranging from housing to overseas chemical plants, architectural services, and civil engineering for roads, bridges, and other such facilities.

Real Estate: The Seoul housing market had not been doing as well as in other cities and provincial areas in recent years. In 2010, however, construction companies began providing discounts on unsold apartments, resulting in greater sales. The South Korean government had also been trying to support the property market by supplying low-end/mid-end apartments to increase supply, reducing or removing tax on owners of multiple homes, and deregulating the reconstruction/redevelopment market to increase the number of new apartments.

Internet Business: South Korea's Internet business was alive and well. Although the online gaming market faced lower growth rates than in the past due to stricter government regulations, the search portals were doing well.

South Korea's strength in such a diverse range of sectors left us confident of the country's bright future.

Chapter Nine

It's Called Volatility

~

What Goes Up Comes Down,
and What Goes Down
Comes Back Up

THE ESSENCE OF HONG KONG is the refinement of risk taking. In the socialist lexicon, assuming even a reasonable level of risk taking is called *speculation*, and is regarded as the root of all evil. But to the committed free marketeer, speculation is a more morally neutral matter of setting your sights on a target in the near future and running a real risk of being wrong but being more confident of being right.

The most lasting lesson I learned during nearly 30 years of living in Hong Kong is the ultimate value of risk taking. The Hong Kong stock market makes an ideal case in point. It's famously volatile, and requires nerves of steel to ride out its hair-raising roller coasters. But from those dark days of 30 years ago, when a good number of Hong Kong fortunes were made by those willing to see a bright future even before seeing the light at the end of the tunnel, I learned that it usually pays to take the long view. In Hong Kong I also learned that all markets are inherently elastic, and that while what goes up always goes down, the converse is equally true.

A Research Challenge

One day in 1973, I got a call from the grandson of the famous Chinese comprador who made millions by being the middleman between Chinese businessmen and the British colonial business establishment. At the time the British Colonial office ruled Hong Kong, Chinese people were not permitted to live high on Hong Kong Island's Peak, but this businessman was allowed to do so because not only of the valuable services he rendered to the British but because of the great wealth he had amassed. I was surprised when he said: "I want to know what's going on in the stock market. I want to know what's going to go up and what's going to go down. Can you give me some research?" I would, I could, and I did.

I approached my new commission as I would have any other market research assignment: by hitting the books. Still a perennial student at heart, I started out studying the technical analysis of price movements using the chartist methodology. The deeper I delved into this arcane art, the more intrigued I became by its possible predictive potential. Of course, this was before I was introduced to value investing and thus my approach now would be considered rather naïve. In any case, that year, 1973, just happened to mark the peak of one of the longest, most aggressive bull runs in postwar Hong Kong history. So, as a fledgling chartist, I was a bit taken aback to discern one of the best-known technical price formations, the famous head and shoulders formation, taking place right there in Hong Kong.

A head and shoulders formation occurs when aggregate stock prices form a top, correct, then run up to a higher top, then retreat and finally come up to a third peak, which is not quite as high as the previous highest top. The line on a graph assumes the shape of a shoulder and then a head, and then falls down to the other shoulder. If you see a head and shoulders formation taking shape on a stock market chart, the chartists say that you should beware and it's probably time to exit and exit fast.

A Painful Lesson

Armed with this ominous information, I filled the Chinese client in on my forebodings. Unfortunately, I neglected to follow my own advice. One too-hot-to-handle stock that an old friend and colleague, was particularly enthralled by was called Mosbert Holdings.

Mosbert was a sprawling, ill-defined Malaysian holding company that had made a mysterious entry into Hong Kong, and despite the fact that nobody could figure out where the money came from, had been noisily, busily buying up everything in sight: companies, buildings—whatever it could get its hands on.

"I bought Mosbert at eight and now it's down to three and a half, half of what I bought it for," my friend excitedly explained, in a somewhat muddled version of contrarian thinking. "It's a fabulous buying opportunity."

Well, maybe yes, and maybe no. Before taking the plunge, I decided to do some minimum due diligence. I picked up the phone and gave the folks at Mosbert a call. The fellow I spoke to was remarkably unfriendly, and to put it mildly, the last thing from an open book.

"I can't give out any information over the phone," he said brusquely. "And nothing's available in print." As if to drive home that point a little deeper, he hung up on me.

Needless to say, I found this all a bit disconcerting. But my friend repeatedly assured me that Mosbert was going to be the next great Hong Kong financial miracle, not to mention, at present prices, the bargain of the century. Against my better judgment, I said, "Let's go for it."

And so we did. Suffice it to say, the slew of cheaply printed Mosbert shares were not worth the paper they were printed on. Not only does a high-flying market cover all sins, it covers all scams. Mosbert Holdings turned out to be one of the biggest scams to emerge from a scandal-ridden Hong Kong stock market, which within weeks was collapsing all around us.

Mosbert, of course, went belly-up. Looking back in anger, we had been complete dolts. We should have wondered why the stock was depressed. The people on the street who had been driving Mosbert stock down knew a few things that we didn't: that Mosbert was not entirely on the up-and-up. We should have held on to our wallets when this publicly listed company refused to provide any information to us about its operations and finances. It was a good lesson on why fundamental value research is so important before making any investment decisions.

And with Mosbert on the ropes, the great Hong Kong bull market had buckled to its knees. From a peak approaching 300 (to put matters in perspective, it previously had hovered as high as 2,500), the Hang Seng index dropped like a stone to less than 100. At that point, it settled into a gradual, steady decline. What was the lesson to be learned from all this? Was it to stay out of volatile markets like Hong Kong? No. As far as I was concerned, the lesson to be learned from this disaster was: What goes down usually goes back up, if you're willing to be patient and don't hit the panic button.

~

**What goes down usually goes back up,
if you're willing to be patient and don't
hit the panic button.**

Don't Forget to Use What You Learn

If you don't follow what you learn, and you don't act on the information that you have gathered, and if you give in too readily to what Alan Greenspan so memorably dubbed the "irrational exuberance" of a runaway bull market, you might end up diving off your own head and shoulders.

At times of distress, there's a tendency to live too much in the moment. Emotions take place in the moment; rationality looks forward and backward in time. Panic and fear—as well as greed—bring sentiment into the foreground and make rationality take an emotional backseat. But examining a subject in the light of history generally helps you take the long view.

Chapter Ten

The Importance of Being Contrary

Don't Follow the Crowd

I CAN HEAR YOU asking: How on earth, when all the smart money was running scared out of Thailand at the height of Asian contagion, could it have possibly made sense to buy there?

For the right answer to a good question, let's take another look at a pet phrase from Sir John Templeton: "To buy when others are despondently selling and to sell

---
~

**"If you buy the same securities as other people,
you'll get the same results as other people."**

—Sir John Templeton

---

when others are greedily buying requires the greatest
fortitude but pays the greatest rewards."

Now, the emphasis here is on the value placed on
an asset by sentiment, as opposed to pure, dispassionate
logic. Despondency and greed are emotions. They aren't
about thinking, but feeling. You may feel in your gut
that a stock is going to go up, but you're better off testing that hunch against the hard-core reality of a corporate balance sheet and such things as the competitive
environment.

Of course, in the short term, the smart money tends
to be right: When the Thai Baht drops by 50% in two
months, you've got a full-fledged disaster on your hands.
But if you sell then, history has shown that your decision
would have been based on sentiment and emotion, not on
a rational assessment of long-term fundamentals.

Of the decisions made by the herd, a certain
percentage will be based on reason, but a far greater
proportion will be based on emotion. So turn the picture

upside down: You earn money by discounting a market's emotional quotient.

Paper versus Realized Loss

Many years ago, my brother's wife bought shares in one of our global emerging markets funds. Her market timing was bad, since she purchased the shares at the height of the 1993 emerging markets boom because everyone else was buying at that time and the news was all positive. We were having an emerging markets boom.

That boom, unfortunately, was quickly followed by the great 1994 emerging markets bust, brought on by the Mexican Peso crisis, which led to the tequila effect, leading to a crash in Latin American markets.

Now, when my sister-in-law saw her monthly fund financial statement she was shocked to find that since the net asset value of her shares had declined, she had "lost" money.

However, even though the assets had declined in value, she hadn't actually lost anything unless for some reason she was compelled to sell at that point. In fact, this was the time of greatest opportunity for her, as well as for me, because for every dollar she invested in our fund during the bust, she was getting more assets for her money.

But for a while there, since she hadn't yet caught on to that fact, you could have cut the atmosphere in her and my brother's house with a knife on the night I stopped by for dinner.

My sister-in-law, being the fine woman she is, didn't hide what she thought under a bushel basket. "It went *down*," she moaned, the first time I saw her after the big drop, in hushed tones, as if the neighbors might hear and think the less of us for our disgrace.

I begged her to have faith, and to take advantage (if she still had the stomach for it) of the marvelous discounts at which she could now buy more shares in my falling fund. She looked at me as if I'd lost my marbles. How could any sane person, she asked, buy into a falling—she might even have said failing—fund?

Because, I explained, "If you buy low now, that gives you an opportunity to sell high later."

This is obvious in its own way, but it's astonishing how many investors do precisely the opposite. Suffice it to say, my sister-in-law bought high and sold low. This is not the way to buy and sell mutual funds or anything else, for that matter.

———————————— ∼ ————————————

Buy stocks whose prices are going down, not up.

If a market is down 20% or more from a recent peak and value can be seen, it's a good idea to start buying.

Sounds crazy, right? Wrong.

Keeping a Cool Head

A case in point: In 1991, one fund company found that Japanese investors were excited about investing in Indonesia so they launched an Indonesian fund for sale to investors in Japan. The launch of the fund coincided with the then peak of the Indonesian market, just prior to a major market meltdown. Of course, no one knew that at the time. However, the fund manager smelled a bubble aching to burst because stock prices were sailing skyward like helium balloons. At the time, because I was in Japan, I asked a Japanese fund manager his strategy for picking stocks. "I select stocks," he solemnly said, "that are going up." This is, of course, a brilliant strategy in a bull market.

But if you get in at the start of a bear market, it's a prescription for ending up with real problems with your portfolio. In any event, examining the hard numbers—the P/E ratios—of the leading Indonesian stocks, the prices being asked relative to the company histories made the whole country look very expensive, particularly in relation to other, rival markets in the region. The fund manager of that Indonesian fund was in a real quandary because the Japanese investors, who had entrusted him with millions of dollars, expected to make a killing in his fund but he was having trouble finding bargains and was looking a bear market in the face. What he did was sit tight. "Hurry up!" investors kept calling and faxing and e-mailing him. "Get invested 100%! If you're not 100% invested you're not earning your fee!" He took the heat, and didn't budge one inch from his stationary position. Shortly thereafter, the bottom fell out of the market, and it didn't take two minutes for those same investors to start calling him up, suddenly singing a different tune: "Stop buying stock! Start selling stock! Stay heavy in cash!" He didn't breathe a word, not even the four famous words: "I told you so."

Nobody ever thanked him, by the way, for saving their skins. But even more to the point, the shareholders began putting pressure on him to *stop* buying just when it made sense to *start* buying. They were frantic about losing their money, but he had to keep telling them, doing his best to keep his exasperation in check: "These short-term losses are only *paper* losses. The only way to *make* money is by buying now." Their problem, of course, was a lack of a proper long-term perspective.

Over more than two decades of emerging markets investing, I've found that being a genial yet cynical optimist is the best posture to earn long-term dividends in

—— ❧ ——

Time heals most ills . . . particularly with regard to emerging markets.

emerging markets. Because despite all the stops and false starts, booms and busts, bubbles and crashes, over the long haul the same logic seems to apply: Time heals most ills . . . particularly with regard to emerging markets.

Chapter Eleven

The Big Picture and the Small Picture

∼

A Case Study of Russia

OFTEN THE BIG PICTURE contradicts the small picture.

I can still recall that when I traveled to Russia looking for investments in the early 1990s, the big picture
was that the place was dirty, low-down, and dishonest.
But the small picture presented isolated pockets of real
opportunity. We're talking macro versus micro views
here. Although Russia's political, economic, social, and

--- ∼ ---

**By correcting the gap between the macro
and micro views, you can get a jump
ahead of the crowd.**

---

financial situations all left a lot to be desired, there were
still bargains to be found.

And by correcting the gap between the macro and
micro views, you can get a jump ahead of the crowd.

The Bad and the Good

When we first began tentatively sniffing around Russia,
the macro picture could not have been more bearish,
unless a full-fledged civil war had broken out.

- A besieged Boris Yeltsin had barely staved off a
  countercoup by shelling the parliament.
- The place was a hotbed of hard-core Communist
  resistance.
- Inflation was skyrocketing.
- Industrial output had hit rock bottom.
- Capital flight was endemic. Any Russian with a few
  rubles to his or her name had smuggled the money
  out of the country and shoved it in some offshore

safe haven far removed from the long arm of the Moscow tax collector.

- There were no well-organized stock exchanges.
- There were no balance sheets.
- There were no earnings reports, because there were no earnings.
- The country was deep into what became known as the Great Contraction, when the country's gross domestic product (GDP) plunged by nearly half in five years.

I could go on; Russia was in a tough spot at the time.

So what attracted us? There was stock to be bought, for nickels and dimes to the share. Companies were being privatized right and left—big ones, small ones, good ones, bad ones, sometimes as many as a dozen a week.

Assets were being auctioned off like excess inventory for pennies on the dollar—or old rubles to new rubles—to sometimes not even the highest but often the *only* bidder. Entire companies—oil and ore giants, telecoms, energy companies—could be had for peanuts.

So why was the Russian state so determined to conduct a fire sale of its potentially valuable assets? The government desperately needed money. And a lot of individuals—mostly managers—also desperately needed money. So they were skimming and scamming and getting rich in the chaos. This made many ordinary people who were excluded from those deals very angry.

But there was also another, more legitimate reason that things were so cheap in Russia back then: No one could be sure which way the wind would blow—toward a viable conversion to a market economy or toward a civil war between would-be capitalists and ardent counterrevolutionaries.

The ultimate big winners of the second Russian Revolution (to convert to a market economy) were by no means clear. So we foreigners, in effect, had to *get paid* to take the plunge. Fortunately, those of us willing to take the risk came out smelling like roses—at least for a while, until the expected and probably inevitable deluge.

"Trust Us"

When we first set foot in Russia, registration of shares was a problem. "Who registers the shares?" we would ask, toward the end of nearly every company visit. "Oh, we do," the company official would smilingly reply. "But what's our guarantee that if you don't like our face, you won't just go and erase our name from the registry?" "Trust us" came the reply. But personally, the lack of a central share registry made me very nervous.

Back in 1994, the Russian Stock Exchange was so primitive that trading began at around three o'clock in the afternoon, give or take an hour or so, when a BMW would pull up to the stock exchange building in Moscow to unload a few million bucks' worth of cold cash.

Brokers would sit at long tables waiting for workers and ordinary citizens who had been given share vouchers—which could be exchanged for shares in newly privatized Russian companies—to bring them in by the bushel and sell them for a song.

At around six o'clock in the evening, the BMW would return to collect the vouchers that the brokers had bought on the cheap from the gullible workers and citizens. As one veteran of the scene recently recalled, "It really was 'over the counter.'"

Fast-forward two years. By 1996, the Russian Trading System (RTS), an electronic link between brokers and dealers established under the aegis of the U.S. Agency for International Development (USAID), was trading an average turnover of the equivalent of US$14.2 million daily.

This wasn't too bad, considering that the vast majority of Russian stocks were still so thinly traded that we had to wait days, or even weeks, to execute a trade.

Five years after we purchased our first Russian stock, the Russian bear boom had entered its second year in high gear. So the same two questions now arose that hover ominously over all runaway booms, at all times, anywhere in the world:

1. Is this the peak before the decline?
2. Or is this the early stages of a prolonged wild party?

There were, on the macro level, a few things to feel good about and to give us confidence that despite all our misgivings, some real and sustainable growth was taking place that would justify those rising share prices.

After plunging 43% since 1989—the year the Berlin Wall came crashing down on the Communists' heads and the Iron Curtain opened like a venetian blind—the Russian domestic economy in 1997 actually reported a marginal gain in GDP of a not exactly staggering 0.4%.

This may not sound like a lot to you, but given the amount of money being made that never got booked, it was mighty impressive—particularly since the GDP had risen for two consecutive quarters, the first such back-to-back upswings in five years. It could have been, for all we knew, the beginning of a Great Expansion—or just a minor blip on the screen.

A Welcome Tidal Wave of Privatization

There had been some impressive—and little-noticed—improvements in the results of that tidal wave of privatization.

Despite the fact that the program had been highly corrupt and much criticized for being riddled with errors, it had accomplished many of its initial goals.

By year-end 1998, 75% of manufacturing enterprises had been privatized, while 85% of manufacturing output was being generated by privatized companies. More than 80% of industrial workers were employed either in privatized or quasi-privatized firms.

Even more critically, the huge industrial overcapacity that had plagued Russia during the Communist era had been largely squeezed out of the now heavily privatized economy. A burgeoning service industry had been created from scratch, with large and small banks, advertising agencies, and shops thriving on the new opportunities.

Under the old system, the prevailing wisdom had been: "He who doesn't steal from the state is stealing from his own children." Another common pearl of workers' wisdom: "We pretend to work, and they pretend to pay us." Taken together, it's not hard to understand why the Soviet system collapsed. In fact, the truly astonishing thing is that it took so long to buckle under its own internal contradictions.

After just a few years of free-market policies, employee morale had sharply improved. "It's become more difficult to steal from new owners than to steal from the state," a Russian oil and gas analyst told the

Wall Street Journal. This fellow attributed the 1.3% rise in oil production in 1998 (not very much but still the first increase since 1988) to the fact that: "Management has become more motivated." In his industry, newly invigorated, financially incentivized managers were "overhauling oil wells, installing new technology, and investing more wisely."

Thank God a few things were going right. From the standpoint of cultural values, the country was in the midst of a major turnaround. A once-insular country, which out of ideological distaste had shunned foreign trade, became a major player in international commerce.

Still, judging by my own personal experience, in too many of these promptly privatized firms, the same old sad socialist sacks were still running the show. This meant, more often than not, running their companies straight into the ground. Five years of high-pressure, full-speed-ahead privatization and economic shock therapy had failed to bring fresh blood into the ranks of too many senior management teams.

If anything, the prospect of getting rich off privatization had encouraged many over-the-hill managers to stay put, hoping to cash in their chips before heading out. As a result, threatened and paranoid managers tended to adopt, in desperation, a passive survival mentality.

This lose-lose strategy involved:

- Lowering output.
- Cutting employment and wages.
- Running up massive arrears to suppliers and the federal budget.

It's Okay to Sell the Crown Jewels

Something, sooner or later, would have to give. The basket of blue-chip stocks held by our Russia Fund had done well. But the investments were getting expensive. The Fund's strategy in Russia in the second year of its boom was the same one that I employ during all booms anywhere and everywhere: Move down the list from the big, large-cap stocks, which have gotten expensive, and look for second-tier companies with small market capitalizations and big growth potential.

Take a good, hard look at your portfolio. Find all the stocks that have gone up 100% or more in one year or less, where the earnings have not risen as much and the five-year projection is not good, and consider dumping them.

⁓

Find all the stocks that have gone up 100% or more in one year or less, where the earnings have not risen as much and the five-year projection is not good, and consider dumping them.

What? Am I nuts? Why sell stocks that are your crown jewels? Because your crown jewel stocks can be your most dangerous stocks. Sure, you feel loyal to them because they've done well by you, and you by them. But watch out. They can be deadly. Let's take a quick look at the situation.

Here it was, a splendid collection of Russian blue chips, nearly every one of which had gone right through the roof—not altogether surprising, in a market that had tripled in value in a mere 18 months. The Fund had a good chunk of:

- The oil giant Lukoil (up 184% in one year).
- Vimpelcom, Russia's number-two cellular phone company (up 154%).
- GUM Trading House (up 132% in one year), the wonderful old department store in Moscow housed in a dramatic location right off Red Square.
- Rostelekom, the huge phone monopoly, and St. Petersburg City Telephone Network, two of the brightest telecom investments available, both well up in the triple digits in the past year.

So I had hit all the sectors and picked up the cream of the crop. I should have been happy, proud as punch. Instead, I was running scared. You don't maintain high

───────── ～ ─────────

**You don't maintain high performance
by holding on to old blue chips that are
no longer blue. Find the next batch
of blue chips before they turn blue.**

performance by holding on to old blue chips that are no longer blue. Find the next batch of blue chips before they turn blue.

The fine, seasoned stocks in our portfolio weren't priceless oils, guaranteed to appreciate forever. They were more like prime steaks, capable of going bad if you held on to them for too long.

As I advised our Russia Fund shareholders after our second successful year in operation: "It's difficult to imagine just how *big* Russia is. If you fly eastward from Moscow, it takes nine hours to reach Vladivostok, on Russia's Pacific coast." Like the United States, Brazil, and China, Russia's *size* is intrinsic to its *character*.

Even after being shorn of many of its Soviet-era and tsarist imperial possessions (and pretensions), Russia is still the largest country in the world, as measured by land mass. It covers nine time zones, stretches nearly halfway across the globe, and contains just about every conceivable form of landscape on earth, from snowy mountains to hot, sandy deserts, from fertile lowlands to dry grasslands, from endless tracts of tundra to lush forests.

Its natural resources are staggering:

- It's the world's largest producer of palladium.
- It's the second-largest producer of platinum after South Africa.
- It's the second-largest producer of diamonds after Botswana.
- It's one of the largest producers of nickel, gold, oil, and natural gas in the world.

On the upside, a big country is a place where companies can grow to fit the landscape. Where the potential domestic markets are huge, companies don't have to rely so much on export-driven strategies to succeed. They don't have to rely on a global strategy to succeed. If they can become category killers in their own country, they're halfway there. And having conquered their own territory (assuming that it's big and diversified enough), moving on to the rest of the world doesn't seem like such a quantum leap.

On the downside, large countries' problems are often tailored to their size. They're not nimble. They're not quick. Unlike a small car or a small country, a big market can't easily turn, or be turned around, on a dime.

One time, I visited a company in Vladivostok, an industrial port city on the Sea of Japan. The firm was struggling, with less than 10% of its potential capacity being utilized. Just three years before, the producer of radio and TV components had been struggling to keep up with orders, because it had enjoyed a solid share of the Russian domestic market.

But no longer. With fierce competition from cheaper Asian imports (many originating in countries located not far from Vladivostok by plane), this company's electronics business was distinctly endangered.

Industry Characteristics Aren't the Be-All, End-All

But the electronic components manufacturer's attitude was positive. The company had established ties with U.S., South Korean, and European firms, and although these alliances had not produced much business—let alone hard cash—the managing director radiated hope, optimism, and confidence.

He was excited, he said, about a contract he hoped to sign soon with a South Korean company that might increase production by 50%. Because his business was fundamentally linked to the global economy, the electronic components manufacturer had been forced to engage with the new global realities. Objectively, in some ways, he was in a difficult place. But subjectively, he was miles ahead of the curve. Another, equally important lesson to be learned from not-so-random encounters is: A strictly industry study of a company's situation can be misleading. A visit on the ground can make the difference.

A strictly industry analysis of a company's situation can be misleading. A visit on the ground can make the difference.

Field Note: Russia

June 2010

The Russian economy and stock market, like those of other emerging markets, have had a remarkable recovery. By June 2010, Russian equities had more than doubled from the recent low in January 2009. Although the Russian economy contracted by 8% in 2009, it was actually expected to grow by 4 to 5% in 2010, supported by export growth.

Some of the companies we visited included:

Beverages: At one of the leading producers of vodka in Russia, I learned that the company had been investing heavily on marketing and promotion to move into the high-end vodka market and increase sales of its premium-brand vodka not just domestically but also internationally. Despite the government's efforts to decrease vodka consumption locally by imposing high taxes on vodka, the firm was of the opinion that the crackdown on illegal vodka producers (accounting for as much as 35% of total production) would help legitimate producers such as itself even though overall consumption was decreasing.

Food: Our next visit was to a food-processing company. The story here was market share growth. The market was very fragmented, and the company was expected to have opportunities to grow organically and inorganically. With the exception of pork, which could have profit margins as high as 40%, the meat-processing business had low margins. There were tax subsidies in place for agricultural producers in Russia that would last until 2012, and those might be extended. The

(*Continued*)

valuations also looked attractive; however, the biggest risk was the high capital expenditure. The company was in massive expansionary mode because credit was cheap and management believed it could gain significant market share.

Information Technology: While visiting an information technology (IT) company, I learned about the progress in Russia's IT services sector. Involved in software development, IT services, and computer hardware for more than 1,000 organizations, including government institutions as well as large public companies, this particular firm was a beneficiary of the government's efforts to upgrade its IT systems.

Overall, it was a very fulfilling trip to Russia, where we continued to learn about the investment opportunities in that market.

Chapter Twelve

Pri·va·ti·za·tion

~

The Trend That Can Bring Huge Opportunities

SO HOW DID PRIVATIZATION help transform markets such as Russia? It sounds like the driest of bureaucratic abstractions. Just say it—*privatization*—and those Latinate syllables literally drag on your tongue. But privatization is much more than an abstraction. It's a revolutionary trend that has been sweeping the world for a number of good reasons, not the least of which is that it is the only way for long-dormant value to be pried out of moribund state industries, which have been black holes for capital instead of generators of it.

This has proven true not only in former Communist and socialist countries, and not only in emerging markets, but in developed markets as well. Great Britain and France made fortunes by privatizing their national phone companies, while achieving better service into the bargain.

Privatization has been the engine driving the lion's share of the world's emerging markets. For example, during the first half of 1997, Latin American stock funds produced some of the world's highest annualized returns. The reason? Stock markets in Brazil, Argentina, Mexico, Venezuela, Colombia, Chile, and Peru were all fired up by a wave of privatizations.

In Brazil, the wholesale shifting from the public to the private sector of several key companies, including Telebras (the national phone company), Eletrobras (the national electrical utility), and Petrobras (the state petroleum company), was big news.

Priming the Pump

Getting in early on newly privatized companies is one of the best ways to benefit from the resulting unlocking of value. Of course, gauging these situations can often be tricky, because some countries (and some central governments)

--- ∽ ---

Getting in early on newly privatized companies is the best way to benefit from the resulting unlocking of value.

---

rig the process to benefit insiders, while others simply bungle it in less venal ways that can result in horrendous rip-offs of shareholder value.

To the institutional investor, visiting companies in the early stages of privatization—generally before the shares become listed on international exchanges—is the next best thing to knowing the future. A comparable step for a small investor is buying the shares locally if there is a local listing early on in the privatization process. If the valuations are attractive, an investment via the initial public offering (IPO) can be a good opportunity.

Privatization allows governments saddled with unprofitable state industries to obtain the level of investment necessary to turn these crippled colossi around. Though the fairy tale of the sleeping frog being kissed by the princess and turning into a prince might be a somewhat romantic analogy, privatization can be almost miraculous in its ability to pry long-lost treasures out of rusty industrial chests to which the state had long ago misplaced the key—the key being incentive, of course. More than money, incentives are the royal road to riches.

Profitable investing in emerging markets demands a close study of the privatization process, because the difference between a good and a bad investment can be simply a matter of timing—buying at the right moment in the privatization process. Getting in early on the privatization curve is the key to riding the wave of the future.

Here's How It Works

Under the classic privatization model, state-owned companies seeking to go private are often told by their governments—which still own them—to go hunting for a strong strategic partner, typically a leading company in the same industry as the company undergoing privatization.

The rationale is to provide the resulting joint venture with the technical and managerial benefits provided by the strategic partner, so that these more often than not antiquated, clunky dinosaurs can be turned into lean, mean high-tech machines.

The oft-heard phrase *strategic investor* was no sweeter music to my ears than the dread term *underwriters*—the latter are the investment bankers who manage the issuing of new shares on behalf of new companies, and they like to set higher prices than I like to pay.

In general terms, my experience with strategic investors has not been terribly positive. Why? Because while a portfolio investor like us is looking to make *money*, a strategic investor is looking to gain *control*.

In most national privatization programs, the national telecommunications companies have been among the first firms to be taken private. That's because the revenue to be raised by selling off the telecom operation can be quite hefty, while the investment required to upgrade the system to international standards is typically so great that only a well-heeled, deep-pocketed strategic partner is going to be up to the task of jump-starting these creaky jalopies and kicking them into high gear.

In the 1990s, in Estonia, for example, the Ministry of Posts and Communications hoped for a partner willing to help upgrade the entire domestic phone system, not just the urban network. This was a potential fly in the ointment, because although it was clearly more profitable to serve the more densely populated urban areas, for political reasons the government could hardly ignore the sizable slice of citizenry who lived out in the countryside, many of whom had been on waiting lists for decades hoping one day to be granted the privilege of having their own phone.

Now let's look a little more closely at this decision, because it's critical to any foreign investor, large or small.

Why is the company often placed under a legal obligation to find a strategic partner? Because, just as the management of any private company looking to sell it would want to buff it up to fetch the highest price, the government's goals tend to be:

- To maximize the proceeds from privatization.
- To curry political favor by improving services.

What usually happens is that the new company gets saddled with the political imperatives of the old company. So the government says to the strategic investor: Let's make a deal. We're going to give you an opportunity to make one heck of a lot of money. But in exchange for this opportunity (which we're going to guarantee for a period of time by extending the monopoly enjoyed by the present company's state-owned predecessor) we've put down two nonnegotiable demands:

1. You're not going to be able to provide service only to the people who can pay a lot.
2. You're going to have to serve everyone, even if that involves taking a few losses.

If all goes well, a well-handled privatization can be a win-win situation for everyone involved, from the government to managers to customers to underwriters (investment bankers) to you and me—foreign investors in general.

Why They're Good Investments

The reason that privatizations (provided you get in on them early enough) tend to make good investments is that a combination of higher investment—from the people who buy the shares *and* from the strategic partner, if there is one—with improved management almost invariably leads to higher productivity. I said *almost* invariably—not always.

Whenever you buy stock in a company, you're placing a bet on that company's long-term prospects. The price of that stock is really just the average of a range of potential buyers' and sellers' opinions of what the shares are going to be worth in the future.

Common characteristics of public-sector telecom companies in emerging or, more so, the frontier markets include low penetration rate, excessive prices for the average citizen, and poor phone service. As mentioned earlier in the book, in the developed countries, we tend to take mobile phone service—or more than 90% market penetration—practically for granted. But in Nigeria, for example, it was 55%, while in Bangladesh it's even lower at 46%!

Privatization offers cash-strapped emerging nations:

- A way to get cash out of their antiquated phone networks, which would take millions to bring up to speed.
- A way to close the telecom gap as quickly and efficiently as possible, at next to no cost to the taxpayer.

Low telecom penetration rates represent high potential growth. (Investors *like* telecom companies that start out near the bottom, because that only enhances their upside potential.)

After telecoms, public utilities usually comprise the next wave of state-owned companies to be privatized. They tend to be vast and unproductive, and need serious money to be upgraded into profitability. But on the upside, once they've got their infrastructure in place, their costs can be pushed lower with good management and their profitability can be pushed up with fair rates.

Utilities may not be sexy, but they can be sleepers. The three big questions to ask with any utility:

1. How subject is it to regulation?
2. If it *is* subject to regulation (and most of them are), how onerous is that regulation?

3. If they're *not* subject to government regulation, chances are that's because they're no longer a monopoly. And if they're no longer a monopoly, the overriding question becomes: Can they stand the heat of competition?

Thus, investing in a newly privatized company can lead to substantial profits since you're getting into the company in its early stages of development. As the company becomes more efficient and productive, profitability and subsequently share prices should increase. So it's always wise to keep a lookout for such companies—especially in frontier markets.

Chapter Thirteen

Boom to Bust

~

How, When, and Why?

WHEN THE ASIAN FINANCIAL flu first broke out with a vengeance in Thailand in the summer of 1997, after years of unrestrained lending on speculative real estate projects, the local banks started to look kind of shaky, at least to impartial outside observers.

Three Warning Signs of a Bust

Here are three of the warning signs, by which you can sometimes tell if a boom—any boom—is about to go bust:

1. *The nation's current account is perilously low.* A current account takes the payments a country must make to outsiders, and compares them to all the revenues it's taking in. If the account is out of balance, that's a bad sign. And if the balance skews way toward the net outflow column, that's when global investors start getting nervous.

2. *Inflation is rising.* If the inflation rate starts rising far and fast in any country, take it as a major red flag because the usual central bank response is to raise interest rates, which could create an economic downturn.

3. *Companies are taking out huge loans in Dollars thinking they could easily repay them when the local currency is healthier.* Companies do this because the interest rates could be lower on foreign currency loans than on loans in their own currency.

— ∽ —

Three warning signs of a bust: perilously low current account, rapidly rising inflation, and huge foreign currency debt.

What Happened in Thailand?

In the case of Thailand, companies took on huge foreign currency debt because the interest rates were lower on Dollar-denominated loans than on Baht-denominated loans. They would take the Dollars they borrowed and buy Baht at a lower price, and rake in the profits on the interest rate differential. It was a great way to make money as long as the Baht remained strong. But any sign that the Baht might weaken would surely bring the whole house of currency cards down. In effect, the entire country was gambling on the strength of its own currency, and in 1997 that gamble was looking a little risky.

The big commercial banks—no doubt tipped off by the central bank in Thailand—were beginning to get an idea that perhaps the Baht was not as strong as had once been thought. And the problem with currency is that any perception of weakness may bring about actual weakness. The more people got the idea that the Baht was in danger of being devalued, the greater the chances that it actually would be.

And what would that do? Well, a devalued Baht would make it much harder for all those Thai companies to pay back all those Dollar-denominated loans, because they would need to make many more Baht to pay back those Dollars. That was terrible news for overleveraged companies—which included some of the largest companies in the country—whose debts in some cases would soon start outstripping their assets. This, in turn, would make the banks even edgier, and make them less likely to extend or roll over these loans, because these banks would be looking at big black holes themselves, in the mirror, and would be trying to call in any and all loans to keep themselves from going under.

Into this tense, anxious pool of people biting their nails, waiting for the other shoe to drop, quietly slipped a group of ladies and gentlemen collectively known as forex traders. As I've mentioned, they're also less kindly known as currency speculators, a term that has caught on because it captures some of the flavor of what they do.

And what do they do? They buy and sell various countries' currencies, of course. Now, there was a time when most major currencies were fixed to the gold standard—last established under the Bretton Woods agreement after World War II. But in 1971, most of the world's industrial powers allowed currency exchange rates to float—which meant that they would be permitted to seek their own level on world markets, and that currencies could be traded against each other just like any other commodity. Still, currency trading remained a relative backwater on the financial scene until the mid-1980s, when a massive increase in the volume of foreign trade caused more and more money to go whirring around the world, constantly being exchanged for local currency when it stopped to buy some goods or services. To get just some idea of the size of growth, daily currency trading turnover soared from US$190 billion in 1986 to an estimated US$1.3 trillion in 1998.

As this market grew, traders—with large lines of credit extended from banks, brokerage houses, and other financial entities seeking to get into what can be an extremely lucrative activity—began speculating on these fluctuating currency rates, aided by computer programs and models that help them trade massive amounts of currency at the blink of an eye. Traders trade on margin and put up only a fraction of the amount of currencies they buy and sell. Thousands of currency traders sitting at computer screens all over the world—some working for banks, others for brokerage houses, still others for companies and central banks—influence with countless buy and sell orders the value of many currencies, which trade much like stocks, bonds, or any other sort of financial instrument.

Still, the central banks of many countries sometimes try—and often fail—to fix the rates at which their currencies are exchanged on global markets against other currencies, in an effort to prop up their own economies. If a government wants to favor exports, it will take steps to let its currency drop so its exports become more attractive. If a central bank wants to stimulate imports it will strengthen its currency by purchasing large amounts of its own currency on currency markets.

When a country sets a price at which its currency can be exchanged against another currency, that's called a *peg*. Pegs—typically measured against a stable reserve currency like the Dollar—became popular in some Asian and Latin American countries seeking to lend stability to turbulent or hyperinflated economies. And sometimes, when the central bank of a country has enough hard currency in reserve to support the rate of exchange it wants to maintain by buying vast sums of it on the open market, these pegs hold. And sometimes, they don't.

When they don't hold, it's usually because the currency traders no longer believe in the price being asked for the currency by the central government of a given country. So what do they do?

A Short-Selling Nightmare

The currency traders start selling it short, which means that they make a bet with somebody else that the price of that currency will fall. What do I mean by the term *short selling*, whether it's a stock or a Baht? I call it "selling

something you don't have at a price that you don't want
to pay."

What short sellers do is:

1. Borrow stocks, or bonds, or currencies, or what-
   have-you from their owners.
2. Sell the shares that they've borrowed, hoping that
   the price will fall.
3. Buy the stock, or currency, back at a lower price
   (if the price does fall).
4. Pocket the difference.

The "shorts"—which is short for short sellers—are
taking the risk and making a bet that the price of whatever commodity they're selling will fall by a given amount
within a given period of time. Where they can get caught
is if the price of that commodity, instead of falling, goes
up—at which point they're forced to come up with the
difference. So it's by no means a win-win proposition.
Sometimes, short sellers end up shorting themselves.

But if enough currency traders start feeling in their
bones that the Thai Baht or Mexican Peso is overvalued
at the current or prevailing rate and that it's destined to
take a dive, all of their actions, taken together, will produce that effect. It's a perfect example of the tendency for
markets, being based fundamentally in psychology—hope

and greed—to create self-fulfilling prophecies. Lo and behold, the currency will drop, which gives the central bank of the country two options:

1. Cave in and let the currency float freely to seek its new natural level.
2. Fight and start spending its currency reserves to defend the Baht, Peso or what their currency happens to be.

And the Baht Tumbles

In the case of the Thai central bank—the Bank of Thailand—on July 2, 1997, the bank decided to abandon the Baht's fixed peg to the Dollar (it was actually not a precise peg, but a so-called trading band, or limited range of rates) and let it float on international currency markets. As expected—though not perhaps by the central bank—the Baht collapsed. Over the next few weeks, in an ill-advised and ultimately futile attempt to bolster the Baht, the Thai central bank spent some US$60 billion (US$23 billion of that borrowed) before throwing in the towel.

After that, the Baht was on its own. And what it did was sink like a stone from about THB20 to US$1 to THB50 to US$1. Those with U.S. Dollar loans thus saw their debts more than double in a very short period of time. When global investors—banks, institutions, money funds, and individuals—saw what was going on in Thailand, which was that the vast majority of companies had Dollar-denominated debts greater than their assets, and the Thai banks and so-called finance companies that had extended those loans were going to be in deep trouble, they did just what global investors always do during a time of crisis: They pulled all their money out before they lost any more of it.

During the ensuing period of currency contagion—so called because the rapid drop of the Baht prompted similarly shaky currencies to fall, from Malaysia to Indonesia—a whole lot of very mad people out there (many of them governing the Southeast Asian countries) began stridently denouncing the currency traders and accusing them of engaging in a conspiracy to ruin their once-high-flying Asian tiger economies.

Chief among the proponents of this conspiracy theory was the prime minister of Malaysia, who, having proudly presided over what for a long time had been known as the Malaysian Miracle, had no desire to go down in history as the man who had presided over the collapse of said Malaysian Miracle.

He became convinced that the huge drops in the Malaysian currency, the Ringgit, were the result of this malicious conspiracy on the part of a lot of devilish forex traders. A Muslim, he even went so far as to denounce this ring as a "Jewish" conspiracy, in part because the most visible and famous currency trader of them all, George Soros, just happened to be Jewish.

If this all sounds somewhat unlikely, you may do well to recall that in the 1960s, when the British Pound sterling was suffering pretty much the same fate, Prime Minister Harold Wilson fiercely blamed a cabal of Swiss bankers he called the Gnomes of Zurich for making his life miserable.

With the Baht locked into a sickening downward spiral, the Thai banks—which were now sitting on huge loans in Baht that were looking a lot less likely to be repaid—promptly cut off all lending, bringing the break-neck economy to a screeching halt. This newfound conservatism was in sharp contrast to previous practice, which had been to lend virtually without restriction to just about anyone, particularly anyone who was anyone—that is, with political or social connections to the military, bureaucratic, business, or government elites.

It's Called Crony Capitalism

They even had a name for that sort of thing: *crony capitalism*. It was invented by a clever U.S. journalist to describe the cozy cartels that rose up in the Philippines under the late, not very lamented President Ferdinand

Marcos. But here it was being used to describe the economic system most favored across Southeast Asia, in which cartels and conglomerates with connections to the government or to the army dominated economic affairs.

In South Korea, they called these cartels *chaebol*. In Japan, they called them *keiretsu* or *zaibatsu* before World War II. In Russia, there was *semibankirschina*, which meant "rule of the seven bankers." The entire theory that a high-growth economy was best controlled by a governing elite composed of military and government officials, banks, corporate honchos, and other favored elite, who popularized the term and the concept of so-called Asian values. That was all very well as long as the governments and economies involved could deliver the goods: high rates of growth. But once the music in this game of musical chairs stopped, the governments—and those officials and cronies who had been raking so much off the top—suddenly found themselves being denounced as crooks and scoundrels.

It emerged that there was no such thing, really, as Asian values. There were just fair, open, and transparent economies, and unfair, closed, and opaque ones.

It's not easy to understand exactly how, when, and why a crisis can emerge. Hopefully, you can now recognize what you're dealing with, so let's move on to learning about how you can benefit from it.

Chapter Fourteen

Don't Get Emotional

—~—

How to Profit from the Panic

SO HOW DOES A panic begin? What really happens? And as an investor caught in the downturn, or someone looking to cash in on the panic, what do you do?

The number one thing that you do is: Don't panic. Panic, after all, is an irrational visceral response to a sense of powerlessness and helplessness, which often comes from a lack of understanding of the actual circumstances. But panics, odd as this may sound, are nothing to be scared of.

As Franklin Roosevelt once said during the Great Depression, "The only thing we have to fear is fear itself." Understanding the origins of the difficulty can help to diminish anxiety. And in any number of critical ways, all busts start with a boom. Why? Because all busts start with a gathering consensus that a market has gone too far, too fast.

The same people who were so in love with the market, and with every stock in it, that they'd sell their grandmothers into slavery to buy more stock, now all of a sudden won't touch a share of stock with a 10-foot pole. Objectively, this fickle attitude makes absolutely no sense. But that's failing to take into account the rule of emotion, which tends to stimulate snap judgments. Emotions make people see only in black and white, good and bad, up and down, so what was good suddenly becomes bad. What do you do in such conditions?

Wait for the panic and the inevitable crash in prices. Then, calmly, buy.

Why? Because you're being paid to take a risk that the short-term sentiment is greatly exaggerated. In the perception gap between emotion and reason, you'll find your buy window.

~

In the perception gap between emotion and reason, you'll find your buy window.

Become a Fan of All the Information You Can Find

Hoping to avoid getting roasted, some stock market crystal ball gazers perform a mathematical ritual known as technical analysis in the hope of forecasting these big market drops.

Such analysis is another aid to understanding what is happening in the market. It is the study of price movements across all kinds of markets, including stock markets. It is different from the fundamental analysis of such variables as price-earnings ratios, profits, earnings, market share, and other factors impacting corporate performance since it focuses only on the stock prices.

As I pointed out, early in my career, when I was working in Hong Kong as a consultant, I started my study of stock markets with technical analysis. From a chartist's point of view, there are certain definable patterns in price movements as put on a chart, which could help us predict what could happen to the price in the future. In the case of the Thai crash, we discussed previously that the chart pattern was what is referred to as a quadruple top, where the market peaked four times before crashing. Such patterns are unusual, since most crashes are preceded by a head and shoulders pattern, as we discussed, or a double or triple top. A quadruple top usually means a severe and dramatic movement, which was experienced in Thailand.

In times of market volatility, to adopt a contrarian position, technical analysis can help the investor find the right times to enter and exit, provided that the value fundamentals are clear. The important point is that when everyone is dying to get in the market, when the stocks are too expensive, it is best to exit—but when everyone is screaming to get out and the stock are cheap, that is the time to buy.

When everyone else is dying to get in, get out. When everyone else is screaming to get out, get in.

The Example of China Telecom

I can still recall the frenzy around the listing of China Telecom in 1997, in the midst of the Asian financial crisis.

The *New York Times* expressed the spirit of the time when it stated: "For investors still willing to try the bumpy ride in Asia, it's hard to think of a sexier pair of words than 'China Telecom.'" (China Telecom was broken up in 1999, and reborn as China Mobile.)

Broker analysts had dubbed the company the hottest "red-chip" initial public offering to come down the pike since the handover, when Hong Kong was returned to China. ("Red chips" are mainland Chinese companies listed on the Hong Kong Exchange).

Even as Hong Kong's financial secretary was publicly insisting that there was "no political or economic need for us to disband the Hong Kong Dollar peg," one of the most renowned Hong Kong stock analysts was blandly assuring us that buying China Telecom was a "no-brainer"—and guaranteed to make money for those who purchased the stock.

"The issue is oversubscribed by 300 times," he bleated, visibly salivating at the very thought. "It's a hot issue. I'd buy as much as you can get. The gray market is saying you'll double your money in one day. It's putting a 100% premium on the market price."

Whenever you hear the words "no-brainer" and "hot issue," it's best to turn on the alarms.

The issue was finally oversubscribed not by 300 times but by 30 times. Two days later, with the Hang Seng index doing a splendid imitation of a lead weight in free fall, China Telecom was set to open at HK$10.00—below the initial offering price of HK$11.68. This highly touted US$4 billion stock offering had promised to be the bellwether for red chips in the post-handover Hong Kong.

But come the fall, the overheated market in red chips had cooled considerably. By Black October, red chips had dropped 40% from their peak in late August. What to do? Well, the first thing I did was have a meeting with some of the top executives at China Telecom. Taken at face value, the numbers looked great.

China Telecom was, according to its glossy prospectus, expertly prepared by the lead underwriters of the initial public offering, "the dominant provider of cellular telecommunications services in Guangdong and Zhejiang provinces which are among China's most economically developed provinces and the two provinces in China with the largest numbers of cellular subscribers." In other words, *la crème de la crème,* cellularly speaking.

Not only that, but the telecommunications industry in China had experienced rapid growth in recent years, and the cellular services sector was one of the fastest growing sectors within the telecommunications industry. In short, what was there not to like? After all, China Telecom's cellular subscriber base had grown at an annual rate of 88% over the previous three years. The strong growth trend was expected to continue, according to management. On top of that—as the stock underwriters had put it in touting the stock—"You're buying an effective monopoly."

Even without all the rocking, rolling, and roiling in Asian markets—which I calmly considered a fleeting epi-phenomenon—buying China Telecom at its high initial offering price was, despite the underwriters' flamboyant assurances, by no means a no-brainer.

This was also despite the gray market placing a 100% premium on the shares—according to rumor. The gray market, incidentally, is a market in shares that have been allocated to certain subscribers at the initial share issue who immediately turn around and sell their share allocation, right out of the gate, to buyers willing to pay a steep premium for the shares before the actual listing.

My little head-mounted antennae were quivering like tuning forks, picking up danger signals. As best I could figure it, China Telecom's assets when compared to similarly situated cellular companies elsewhere in the world were being valued at a very high price.

Of course, for everyone involved, buying this stock meant placing a bet on the future. For my purposes, I wasn't as concerned about today's price-earnings ratio as I was about those five years down the line. But for that price-earnings ratio to be any kind of bargain in five years' time, China Telecom's growth in revenues—as opposed to subscriber base—would have to be staggering. And even then, growth in numbers or market share wasn't the point. It was growth in profits that mattered.

To their credit, I found the managers of China Telecom impressive. And I had not the slightest doubt that under such obviously capable management, China Telecom would flourish in its local market. But I did harbor some doubts about the company's long-term revenue growth prospects. Simply put, as cellular phone service becomes more of a mass medium, prices—and possibly profits—were bound to go down.

The looming question was: Would increased volume compensate for the drop in revenue per subscriber? Add to that uncertain mix the feeding frenzy that typically accompanies these red-chip initial public offerings, and my gut response was rank skepticism.

When an initial public offering is oversubscribed, this means that more people—institutional and retail investors—have put in their bids (and in many cases written sizable checks for shares they hoped to buy) than will ever lay hands on the shares.

China Telecom's underwriters had been granted the right by the company to essentially allocate the shares as they saw fit, which meant that a certain (small) percentage would go to New York in the form of American depositary receipts (ADRs), and a certain (higher) percentage would be listed in Hong Kong.

Initial public offerings are intrinsically unfair, insofar as both share underwriters and the company are permitted a wide degree of latitude in granting preferential treatment to most favored customers. With a "hot" one like China Telecom—piping hot until the day the bottom dropped out of the Hong Kong stock market—the gray market quickly bid the price way up above the initial share, or opening, price.

A Chance for Small Investors

The gray market is made up of all sorts of frustrated buyers who, because they haven't been given a share allocation, promise to pay a substantial premium to any people who did get their hands on some shares over the official market price, if they will sell their shares to them.

This means that anyone who's lucky enough to get a chunk of stock on the first round—a privilege bestowed sometimes by random lottery, and at other times because of connections to the underwriters—can simply turn around and flip the stock, minutes after that investor bought it, into the gray market and make a tidy profit in no seconds flat.

One factor influencing the so-called gray marketeers is the expectation that the new share issue will soar like a hot-air balloon. What I often do in initial public offerings is hang back and wait to see what happens to the shares in the aftermarket—that's the open market—in a few weeks or months. Of course, there's no way to be sure that the price will drop, but once the initial euphoria has ended, it's not uncommon in my experience for initial public offering prices to dip, or at least drift, once the support limits promised by the first round of buyers have been breached.

In any given share allocation scheme, a certain proportion of the total shares issued is guaranteed to be sold to the general public. So it's perfectly possible for small investors to participate in an initial public offering.

Chapter Fifteen

Turning Fear into an Advantage Instead of a Disadvantage

---~---

A Case Study of Thailand

LET'S TAKE THE THAI people. I'd lived in Thailand for a few years, back in the 1960s, and I'd been back quite a few times in the years since. I thought I knew the Thai people pretty well, and I had great respect and admiration for them. In particular, I respected them for their capacity to persevere in times of adversity and smile when things got difficult.

~

When everyone else is getting all pessimistic, that's usually when it is time to turn optimistic.

Something that people tend to forget is that during times of panic, adversity often brings out the best in people. And, by the same token, prosperity often brings out the worst in people.

Within a matter of months, not years, after the Asian financial crisis, I could see the progress that the Thai people and the formerly stagnant Thai government had made to set things right. It takes a major blowout for tectonic plates to shift.

The boiling point had come when the embattled prime minister seriously suggested that the economy could be saved by opening up more Thai restaurants and popularizing Thai kickboxing.

It took just a few serious protests in Bangkok—mounted not by disgruntled leftists and radicals, but by sober, dark-suited businesspeople, middle-class people feeling the pinch and getting hopping mad about it—to suddenly result in a new government and a new, more respected prime minister. The king had stepped in and started to exert moral pressure to lessen corruption and self-dealing on the part of the local elites. Would all these bad people all of a sudden turn into angels? Of course not, but for a while at least, it would behoove them to keep their noses clean. That, in time, would help revive morale and bring the market around.

The people get it together. They start pulling together. They clean up their acts, and start demanding that people in charge do the same. They start working harder. They start saving more. They stop spending money. This was what Oliver Wendell Holmes meant when he spoke of "the moral equivalent of war."

As a partner in the Bangkok office of a consulting firm said during the depths of the crisis: "Even turkeys can fly in a hurricane. But when the wind dies down, it's much more difficult to sustain performance. It's a question of muscle."

He soberly added, "During a downturn, you need to not just cut fat. It's even more important to start building muscle." This means that sooner rather than later, the situation begins slowly but surely to turn around.

Going for Liquidity

The first thing to do in times of crisis is go for liquidity. You could call it a flight to quality. It only stands to reason that if I now have a choice between a small *illiquid* stock and a large *liquid* stock, I'll pick a liquid one every time. In fact, the only time that I buy illiquid or less liquid stocks is if I have to—during booms, when liquid stocks get too expensive.

The first thing to do in times of crisis is go for liquidity.

Liquid stocks tend to be the market leaders, large-cap stocks, index stocks, and blue chips—the stocks you can never buy during a boom, but are your first choice at the first sign of a bust. As sentiment sours, these stocks will begin to come down to more reasonable levels.

In Thailand, I was aching to take a closer look at Siam Cement, one of the country's blue-chip companies, partly owned by the royal household. This was more than just a cement company, but a diversified group with holdings in building materials, petrochemicals, plastics, and a number of other basic building-block raw chemical materials.

It was getting a bad rap in the press: exports down, plants being closed. In other words, now was the perfect time to pay a visit. Was Siam Cement, you might ask, one of those companies that irresponsibly took out loans in dollars with the expectation that they could be paid back in Baht? Well, yes. And, I ask you, so what?

The point is, they all did it. The point is, such a strategy seemed sound at the time. In fact, the fact that Siam Cement was widely known to have suffered that exposure made it worth buying. Why? Because these ideas about exposure to risk tend to weaken sentiment, which makes them attractive targets.

With the currency devaluation, the beleaguered Baht would soon be looking competitive again. Under pressure to increase business through exports, Siam Cement was going to start exporting like crazy, because it could make and sell cement and all of its other products more cheaply than its competitors in neighboring countries could.

And Thailand, which had slapped an export tax on cement, had—lo and behold—canceled that tax for the duration. This made Siam Cement even cheaper to the Malaysian market—even cheaper, in some cases, than Malaysian cement. So, like a kid in a candy store, I was rarin' to start buying up all those juicy blue chips I couldn't afford before the crash.

Playing Pin the Tail on the Bottom

As the Asian virus raged ominously throughout the continent, the new verbal game being played out grimly in global financial circles became "pin the tail on the bottom."

One global trader announced that this wasn't a panic, but "a systematic meltdown of testing a new bottom." Say what? Other self-styled experts pronounced this a terrific time for "bottom fishing." Still others spoke loftily about "breaching the quadruple bottom."

Meanwhile, into the breach plunged the intrepid International Monetary Fund, the global institution best equipped to deal with such crises of confidence. It promptly stepped up to the Baht with a generous offer: a US$17 billion bailout and rescue package, which was dangled like a carrot in order to force the ruling elite to swallow the harsh medicine of financial discipline.

But, in the short term, sentiment was so sour that even the prospect of powerful external forces leveraging the Thai economy back into line did little to raise morale.

Hoping to steal a leaf out of my own book, I hopped onto the next flight to Bangkok. Now how on earth, you might ask, could we be the slightest bit optimistic about Thailand when all the smart money was deserting the place, as if the country had contracted the plague?

The main reason that we felt positive was because all of the trends were so negative. This was not just to be stubbornly or rigidly contrarian—because being a true contrarian means not to go slavishly against the grain, but to be always independent in your thinking. It was simply that we and the short-term smart money were operating according to different time frames.

A Rosier Outlook

In the short term, the smart money was right on the money. For the near future, Thailand was a mess. But over time—I reckoned three to four years, maybe five at the outside—precisely because things were going to get so tough, the Thai people would change their behavior dramatically. Here's how (and why):

- They would not borrow as much.
- They would not buy as much.
- They would save more.
- They would work harder.
- They would break their necks to export because they would need dollars.
- Their industrial output would increase.

And last but not least, not by a long shot:

- They would demand more from their government by way of reform.

And they did. The case study of Thailand is just one example of how the only thing to fear is fear itself. And, in actuality, fear can be used to the investor's advantage time and time again.

Chapter Sixteen

The Crisis Bargain Bin

~

Taking the Long-Term View in the Aftermath of a Crisis

WITHIN JUST A FEW months of the start of the Thai crisis, Thailand showed some measurable improvement in a couple of key areas. An irate citizenship forced government changes so that a new, more forceful administration came in. The new government administrators who took over were praised by everyone we spoke to. They generally agreed that they were the most talented group to run the country in a long time. That alone gave me hope for growth.

Tough times bring leaders to the fore. An apt analogy would be Franklin Roosevelt's famous first 100 days, when the New Deal was ushered in to help rescue the country from collapse.

Only in times of crisis will people change their destructive behavior patterns. Only when there's a consensus that something is broken will anyone take the trouble to see that it gets fixed.

Many Bangkok blue chips enjoyed pride of place in our portfolio as jewels in our crown and, at the right price, deserved a larger place. It was time to focus on those bargains and winnow out those companies that could not survive and prosper in the new environment. It was time to buy some stocks and sell some stocks, reasonably, rationally, prudently and cautiously. Someone asked me how I was purchasing Thai stocks. My reply: "Like porcupines make love . . . with great care!"

No Pain, No Gain

Looking at the macro picture for the near term, things could not have been much worse. However, from my point of view, that was not altogether a bad thing, because we trade in perceptions as much as reality. When we're hunting for bargains, we look for stocks that look lousy but are in fact simply being misjudged. By the end of 1997, the Thai stock index had declined 70% from its all-time peak.

In 1993, at the height of the Southeast Asian boom, the total market capitalization of the Thai stock market had been US$133 billion. By early 1998, it had declined to a dismal US$22 billion.

From my point of view, even with the index down in the dumpster, there had to be more than a few treasures that were being tarred with the same brush. The Stock Exchange of Thailand index's calamitous drop clearly indicated that the average investor in Thailand currently regarded Thai stocks as poor bets.

If we'd been looking at the same group of stocks from the same short-term perspective, we, too, would probably have cut our losses and run. But as we saw it, the market was once again overshooting the mark, and opening up for us a rare window of opportunity for increasing our positions in many companies formerly too rich for our blood.

Given the magnitude of the market's decline, you did have to wonder: Could the index go down to zero? In my opinion, the answer was: Not very likely. This was not, I'm afraid, due as much to sound fundamentals as to the sheer volume of money being pumped into the country. The initial US$17 billion injected by the International Monetary Fund to shore up the country's foreign currency reserves was, we assumed, just the first installment of a program that would in time stabilize the currency.

It was not nearly enough money to shore up the country's ailing financial system, but was mainly a stopgap measure to plug the holes in the dikes to stanch the flow of funds leaking out.

The chance that the Thai index would decline an additional 50% before stabilizing, much less recovering, had to be considered. But when stacked up against the far greater likelihood of a gradual if erratic recovery, I held out for the chance of recovery—sooner, rather than later. This issue was of more than academic concern to us, because we'd been sniffing and snooping around and shifting stocks in Thailand since the market took its first big 40% drop. And because we'd been buying stocks aggressively on the way down, that meant that as the market kept dropping, we were losing money hand over fist—on paper, at least.

In what country, I was asked time and time again during the crisis, did I see the greatest bargains? Without hesitation, I'd reply: "Thailand."

If you're savvy enough to buy stocks on the way down instead of on the way up, you need to be willing to rack up losses in the short term. But at certain strategic points

---

You've sometimes got to take some pain in the short term in order to outperform in the future.

in time sometimes you've got to take some pain in the short term in order to outperform in the future.

A Few Cardinal Rules about Timing

The best rule about timing is not to do it. Market timing is not a very fruitful investment technique since it is so difficult to do successfully. Although we generally discourage trying to time the markets, during extreme meltdowns a few cardinal rules do apply. One is that a market in free fall will tend to hit bottom and then rebound as much as 30% before collapsing again.

Why? Because markets generally pick up to a point where spooked investors who've been holding off on selling because they want to keep their losses to a minimum are ready to take their hits and move on.

When buying stocks during a bust, you need to make sure that you're picking long-term recovery prospects, not corpses shortly to be found not on an action list but on a watch list.

Prowling through Bangkok's back streets and alleys and chugging along congested highways lined with half-empty skyscrapers looking for bargains was a bit like panning for gold in a stream of worthless sand. A better analogy might be hunting for diamonds in a bucket of zircons, because although there were quite a few superficially attractive companies out there, too many—if you dug a little deeper or read the fine profit and loss (P&L) print—were deceptively attractive, as opposed to genuinely undervalued.

The two big booby traps, as I saw them, that tend to make trouble during any bust are:

1. Excessively high levels of dollar-denominated debt.
2. Management shock: higher-ups prone to deep denial and/or suffering from what I like to call "deer frozen by oncoming headlights" syndrome.

For example, of the 480 companies listed on the Bangkok Stock Exchange, about 40 had already gone belly-up by year's end 1997. An equal number of sick companies had seen trading in their shares suspended out of fear that if they were traded they, too, would fail. By our calculations, we expected at least another 20 companies to go under before the situation stabilized. We had to keep our eyes out for weak companies and for companies exposed to those companies that wouldn't survive. Although we don't mind losing money in the short term, we don't like it when stocks we own self-destruct in a puff of smoke—and mirrors.

Scoping Out the Banks

So where did we start our search for bargains? The financial sector. Why? Because that's where the damage was perceived to be the greatest and where recovery could come the fastest.

If you watch a bank like a hawk, you'll see in the patterns of its lending practices a blueprint of the macro picture.

———————————— ∿ ————————————

If you watch a bank like a hawk, you'll see in the patterns of its lending practices a blueprint of the macro picture.

During a downturn, banks are always the first to take the hit, and usually the first to recover. Banks, as lenders to individuals and businesses that either can or cannot pay them back, are the canaries in the coal mine of any economy. Coal miners used to carry canaries (in cages) down into deep mines, as early-warning signals of any dangerous level of toxic gas. Since canaries are more sensitive to toxic gas than humans, they'd keel over at the first whiff of gas, long before any coal miner would be affected. Banks, despite their often bloated size, are highly sensitive gauges of any economy, assuming you know how to read the dials. Investors call them proxies for the economy at large.

In times of uncertainty, banks make excellent catchall stocks, because if you buy a piece of a bank, you're buying a piece of every loan on its books, which subsumes the whole economy. Let's say you learn that a bank is pulling back in a certain sector. That could be a sign of weakness in that sector and it will be necessary to investigate carefully before investing. But if you find out that a bank is suddenly extending itself to service a certain sector at a time of widespread distress, that means the bank has found some bright spots in an otherwise dismal picture.

Bankers tend to get a bad rap whenever things turn really sour. Think of the international banker as a guy with a monkey wrench who mans the valves through which money flows, like oil in a pipeline. When times are good, he opens the valves. When times turn bad, he tightens up or even shuts down the valves. With the flow of money frozen, he starts hunting down everyone and anyone capable of funneling some of that money back into the tank. During the sad, sordid saga of Southeast Asia in the late 1990s, international bankers poured some US$400 billion into the region—excluding substantial loans to Hong Kong and Singapore—before abruptly shutting off the valves, throwing the debt engine into reverse, and leaving the poor rejected countries gasping for air. "There was a huge euphoria about Asia and Southeast Asia," a spokesman for one of Germany's major banks admitted to the *New York Times*. "It was *the* place to be."

The problem is always that when the going is good, it tends to be great. But when it gets bad, it gets horrid. International flight capital—money that can be moved in and out of a market at a moment's notice—is poured in at the first sign of strength, and yanked out at the first sight of weakness. What disturbed even the most hard-core free marketeers in the financial community about the Asian contagion was the deadly speed with which this money tap could be turned on and off and, what's more, turned into a kind of financial vacuum cleaner, sucking its victims dry. When the taps get turned off, it's like a deep freeze: No one can budge until the guy with the wrench turns the tap on again.

Another reason to invest in banks when a declining currency is bound to stimulate exports is that it is an easy way to benefit from the growth in exports and how that growth will impact the entire economy positively. There can also be opportunities to benefit from the direct export sector.

A prime example was Delta Electronics, a diversified manufacturer of electrical components whose products would at that point in time have been 50% cheaper than they had been six months before, making their prices highly competitive. Delta was an excellent company, well managed, with a profit growth of 20% for the year. But Delta was also one of a handful of Thai companies clearly in a position to benefit from the currency collapse, and had therefore seen its shares soar 150% since the devaluation of the Baht six months before. But soon Delta was too expensive and it was necessary to turn to the banks. I was more inclined to buy the banks, because—contrary to popular perception—this would be the most efficient way to make an export play, because the banks were financing the exporters. When an entire country goes bad, sentiment usually quickly sours on the banks. But all the banks, one could safely presume, in a position to do so would be doing what Thai Farmers Bank affirmed as its policy: shifting the bulk of its loans from importers to exporters.

The shares should in time reflect the gathering strength of the export-driven recovery. But we were also on the lookout for export plays that were not quite so painfully obvious as electronics.

Looking for Patterns

One key point to always keep in the forefront of your mind while suffering through the bust end of the boom-and-bust business cycle is that the first country to get hit, and hit hard, is typically the first one to recover.

—— ∽ ——

The first country to get hit, and hit hard, is typically the first one to recover.

A corollary to that: The country hardest hit is forced to confront the deepest root causes of its problems, and will therefore be forced to improve its behavior most dramatically in order to attract now-edgy global investors.

Economic recoveries are no different from any other form of recovery: They follow a classic trajectory of a high high, a low low, and an upturn that could be dramatically rapid.

Thailand had gone on a binge—which in this case had been to gorge itself on cheap credit—and was now going to have to go cold turkey. But it didn't pay to sit on the sidelines in Asia and do nothing while waiting for the storm to blow over. In my opinion, it always pays to take direct action. Reason: Stock markets move before the economy. Stock markets anticipate that economic movement is coming in a year or two.

Chapter Seventeen

Overcoming Irrational Market Panic

~

Learning to Be Objective

IF THE WORLD NEEDED any greater proof that globalization was (1) here to stay and (2) a force to be reckoned with, the negative impact displayed by Latin American markets in the wake of the Asian crisis supplied it in spades. On a morning in late fall 1997 after we checked into our hotel on Rio de Janeiro's Copacabana Beach, the high-flying Rio stock market took a stomach-churning 15% tumble, prompted by desperate doings in far-off Hong Kong. That same morning, a sickeningly swift 10% drop on the São Paulo exchange in the first four minutes of the session forced the governors to halt trading for the first time in the exchange's history.

Riding the Rio Roller Coaster

The steepest declines were racked up by a series of high-flying Brazilian blue chips that had enjoyed an average 93% climb in the first nine months of 1997. Anchoring the group were the three prime poles of the Brazilian privatization tripod: Telebras, the state-owned telecom company, Eletrobras, the state-owned electrical utility, and Petrobras, the state-owned oil and energy company. With the Bovespa (Brazilian Stock Exchange index) dropping like mercury in an ice storm, it looked as if the second-best-performing stock market in the world (after Russia) was heading full-speed into a brick wall.

So why were global investors getting so hot and bothered over Latin America, when the currency crisis appeared to be confined to Asia, half a planet away? One easy answer, as well as a true one, was that the whole world was now so intricately interconnected that it was no longer possible to buffer any one market from the behavior of others due to distance alone. Just as chaos theorists had proposed that a butterfly flapping its wings on one side of the earth could cause a hurricane to break out on the other, the slightest trembles and tremors in one financial market could easily infect and influence the others, even if their commercial connections were rather remote. Of course, markets also move in their own directions, one often markedly different from the other.

First-Class Buying Opportunities

How does that affect the investor? Here's how: These global perturbations often present an unprecedented wave of first-class buying opportunities. When markets overshoot and undershoot due to irrational factors, that's when a cool head can win.

If market sentiment suddenly sours on an entire country mainly because it's *perceived* to be linked to problems elsewhere, that sentiment may be a function of *irrational panic*, not *cold calculation*.

In the same way, if sentiment sours on a whole country when individual companies inside that country are still doing well, you can find bargains in stocks that are artificially depressed because of no other reason than popular knee-jerk reactions to temporary events.

With most emerging markets overexposed to the ins and outs and ups and downs of flight capital—money that can be moved in and out of a market at a moment's notice—it's critical to figure out whether these sudden panics (as well as flights of irrational exuberance) are justified by the fundamentals. Because if they're not, betting against them can be your ticket to ride.

Let's take Brazil, for example; the swift transformation from a mixed to a market economy that Brazil pushed itself through during the five years prior to 1997 had set the pace for a regional record 5% growth rate in Latin America in the 1990s, and a record US$45 billion in direct foreign investment flowing into the region as a whole.

In Southeast Asia, the forex traders' alleged collective decision to attack a currency—otherwise known as short selling that currency, with many individual players placing the same bet that it would wilt under pressure— sent a signal to less-plugged-in investors that possibly a few things were rotten in the underpinnings of the so-called Asian miracle—things like rampant corruption, insider dealing, and a lack of transparent markets. That behavior sent those markets into a tailspin, but it would have been realistic, not masochistic, for government officials of Malaysia and Indonesia to bless those currency traders, not curse them.

Why? Because by shining their harsh speculative spotlights on the flagrant weaknesses in their economies, the forex folks were expertly diagnosing precisely what ailed them. Those governments didn't need to hire high-priced consultants, because the currency traders were doing the job for free, with the icing on the cake being a quick profit if their bets went the right way.

But what about Latin America? The prospect of Asian contagion infecting Latin America was like a golden door swinging wide open for bargain hunters, because the supposed links between these two vibrant regional economies were not nearly so strong as popular opinion would have it. Yes, these countries did trade together, and did compete as exporters of goods to more mature markets. But just because they shared some superficial similarities didn't make Latin America just like Asia. If anything, the two continents were growing less alike than ever before.

When the raft of Brazilian blue chips took their first real nosedive in a decade, mainly due to trouble in Asia, I felt in my bones that we were looking at a phenomenon known as *spooking*.

When the ordinary run of buyers gets spooked, that's the time to step up to the plate and start putting your money down on the table.

When the ordinary run of buyers gets spooked, that's the time to step up to the plate and start putting your money down on the table.

Here We Go Again

A major reason that global investors were up in arms over Latin America, after those same markets had doubled, on average, over the previous six months, was that some of the same sins—low or negative current account balances, high foreign trade deficits, creeping inflation—that had brought the Asian tigers low were running rampant in Latin America.

Brazil was more vulnerable to being downgraded in investors' books than its neighbors were, because its currency—the Real—was widely regarded as at least 30% overvalued. But it was important to recognize that although the prospect of a currency devaluation—either abrupt or gradual—represents currency risk in action, a devalued currency can be a country's saving grace, because gradual, panic-free devaluations can kick exports through the roof.

Some simplistic strategies would have you bail out of a country at the slightest hint of a devaluation coming down the pike, because the same share of stock will be worth that much less, in Dollar terms, once the currency declines. But I see things differently. Combined with the negative sentiment that such a prospect represents, I view signs of an impending devaluation as a possible signal to buy into a country—because even if the markets do pull a temporary nosedive, the eventual bounce-back will be all that much stronger than before.

In Rio, the first casualty of the currency traders' preliminary skirmishes was the confidence of local stock traders, who found themselves caught with their pants down by a wave of frantic short selling in anticipation of the coming currency crisis. As one young Rio derivatives trader gloomily observed to the *New York Times* on the morning of the crash (euphemistically called by some brokers a "correction"): "What can I say? Brazil today is no-man's-land. The future is cloudy and stormy, and everyone around here is concerned and desperate. Everything here is so exaggerated. Brazil is a land where death comes suddenly."

Talk about an upbeat assessment!

From my point of view, reading words like these in a daily newspaper was like being handed an engraved invitation to a party. If Sir John Templeton said it once, he said it a thousand times: The right time to buy is always at the point of maximum despondency. Well, here we were at rock bottom, and I was drawing up a shopping list the length of my arm.

Having just left Thailand (which I would have nominated as the global capital of pessimism), it now seemed as if Brazil might be a contender for that dubious distinction.

Among the many reasons being proffered in the press to back up the purported link between Brazil (and Latin America in general) and the problems besetting Asia was that South Korean banks, when the going was good, had bought scads of high-yield Brazilian Brady bonds and would now be forced to dump them on the open market, at fire sale prices, in a desperate bid to raise cash. (Brady bonds, incidentally, were an innovation devised by U.S. Treasury Secretary Nicholas Brady of the Bush administration, by which the U.S. government backed emerging market debt, permitting such countries to borrow on international markets at lower rates.)

Though the Brazilian-Korean bondfire sounded fine on paper, personally I wasn't buying it. For one thing, the amount of money involved, when compared to the size of Brazil's economy, was inconsequential. Another supposed connection between Brazil and troubled South Korea was that South Korean producers were going to start flooding the world with cut-rate cement. Although not entirely off the mark, the adverse effect on a single industry was hardly sufficient to justify the downgrade of a whole country, much less a full-scale market stampede.

It's important to realize that when a panic starts, it takes only the slightest hair-trigger to turn a run into a rout. It can be cement, Brady bonds, or bubblegum—it doesn't matter. The reason for turning tail could even be a missing millionaire. On our second day in Brazil, a completely unfounded rumor that a major Mexican industrialist had disappeared—presumed kidnapped, or even killed—sent shock waves through the region's capital markets. Just as inanely, they promptly bounced back once it was disclosed that the rich gent in question was alive and kicking.

Korean-owned Brazilian bonds, cut-rate Asian cement, and allegedly abducted industrialists all provided jumpy investors with the lazy-headed excuse they were looking for to start dumping Brazil big-time. When things are looking lousy from any number of angles, the collective unconscious always starts snooping around, looking for evidence—no matter how far-fetched—to bolster its depressed emotional state. And that's just the time, as a savvy investor, that you should start taking a serious look at the country.

If the whole world is down on a country for exaggerated, short-term reasons, think of shifting it from a hold to a buy.

If the whole world is avoiding a country for exaggerated, short-term reasons, think of shifting it from a hold to a buy.

Note: You can take advantage of rumors like the missing industrialist by snapping up stock during the moment's downturn, and riding the shares back up north when the smoke clears. But this sort of market timing is a risky, hair-raising strategy—not a move for the novice player or an investor most interested in maintaining a long-term investment horizon.

Don't get me wrong. There *were* more than a few superficial similarities between Asia and Latin America. Like South Korea and like Thailand, Brazil's once-red-hot export growth had been slowing to a crawl all through the fall, a slowdown that had spread to other Latin American economies. The country's current account balance was starting to look like the credit card bill of a confirmed shopaholic. But in contrast to Thailand, where the government had proved ludicrously ineffective in staving off the alleged forex traders' assaults, Brazil's popular president, Fernando Henrique Cardoso, was determined not to let that shadowy crowd get the best of him. If they wanted to fight, he was more than willing. In fact, for better or for worse—personally, I felt for worse—he was willing to defend his currency to the political death, if need be.

Facing Reality

Unfortunately for his citizens, who would soon start feeling the heat, President Cardoso had an election coming up. So he had to act, and act fast. The 66-year-old president knew better than anyone that if the Brazilian Real—which he had personally created—were to start heading south, he would be hitting the South Polar ice cap right along with it. In short, the man's credibility was on the line.

The only problem I had with Cardoso's tough-it-out strategy was that there are times when a devalued currency can kick a failing economy back into high gear, by jump-starting exports. Preventing a currency devaluation can have as much to do with salvaging national pride as with hard-core economic reality. When, in January 1999—shortly after his reelection—he was forced to let the Real float freely, the Brazilian market surprisingly soared. Why? Because the markets were finally forcing the Real to face reality.

Field Note: Brazil

February 2011

Brazil's economy was doing very well. After the contraction in 2009, there was a dramatic recovery in 2010, resulting in a growth rate of 7.5%. Moreover, both inflation and unemployment were

(Continued)

at half the high levels experienced in 2003. Foreign reserves stood at over US$300 billion, up from only US$50 billion in 2006.

One of the big worries was the strengthening exchange rate of Brazil's Real, which had moved from the 2002 low of close to R$4 to US$1, to the current rate of R$1.7 to US$1. Nevertheless, exports were booming on the back of a growing global demand for Brazil's iron ore and agricultural goods. The stock market had also recovered from its recent low in November 2008, returning more than 300% in U.S. Dollar terms as of the end of February 2011.

During our trip to Brazil, we gained insights from a number of companies.

Transportation: The upcoming Olympics and World Cup were expected to benefit companies in the transportation industry. At a leading bus manufacturer, revenues were up almost 50% in 2010, while margins had also improved significantly. In addition to holding more than 40% of the domestic market share, the company had a significant international presence with exports to more than 60 countries.

Agriculture: Brazil's favorable climate and soil as well as relatively cheap labor bode well for agricultural companies in the country. Further-more, high soft commodity prices had been sup-porting earnings in this industry, and I expected this trend to continue. One of the companies I visited reported good earnings on cotton as a result of the high global prices. The three most important variables for these businesses were the cost of raw materials (fertilizers and chemicals), selling prices, and the exchange rate of the Real to the U.S. Dollar.

Natural Resources: Another beneficiary of high commodity prices, natural resources was another sector in which I was interested. Management at a steel company mentioned that although steel continued to suffer margin contraction, the company had been able to deliver above-average results because of its iron ore mines as well as its limestone and dolomite resources in the mineral-rich state of Minas Gerais. This well-diversified company also engaged in cement production since it had dolomite, limestone, and slag from steel operations.

These visits and others I made in Brazil indicated a favorable business environment with continued growth.

Chapter Eighteen

The World Belongs to Optimists

Golden Investment Attributes and Rules

IN EMERGING MARKETS INVESTMENT, I believe it is necessary to be optimistic. The fact remains that there have always been problems and there will continue to be so in the coming years throughout the world. But we are entering an era that is perhaps unparalleled in the history of mankind. With higher income and living standards, better communications and technology, improved travel, greater international trade, and generally better relations between nations, emerging markets investors have the perfect opportunity to capitalize on the benefits.

Studies have shown that stock market investments made in a patient and consistent manner will invariably grow, since there is a natural tendency for the value of equity investments to rise in order to keep up with inflation. In addition, independently managed businesses, competing successfully in the marketplace, are generally winners in the stock markets as there is a tendency for their sales, profits, and assets to expand. However, it is not always possible to predict whether a company is going to be successful or unsuccessful, so it is necessary to diversify.

∿

"The world belongs to optimists. The pessimists are only spectators."

—*François Guizot*

While one can certainly learn numerous technical skills that help in making investments or managing a portfolio, a large percentage of investing is still psychological. Both buyers and sellers act on a combination of instinct, information, and logic. The development of certain personal characteristics could play a key role in contributing to your investment success.

Here are a few key personal attributes that can make for good investment results. These include: discipline, hard work, humility, common sense, creativity, independence, and flexibility.

Work Hard and Be Disciplined

Someone asked me once if I could condense into five words the most important qualities needed for a good investor, and I replied: "Motivation, humility, hard work, discipline." It stands to reason that the more time and effort that are put into researching investments, the more knowledge that will be gained and wiser decisions made.

Be Humble

Humility is needed so you are able and willing to ask questions. If you think you know all the answers, you probably don't even know the questions. As Sir John Templeton once said, "If we become increasingly humble about how little we know, we may be more eager to search."

Show Some Common Sense

To me, common sense is most important when making investment decisions, since the words *common sense* imply the clarity and simplification required to successfully integrate all the complex information with which investors are faced.

Get Creative

I think a significant amount of creativity is required for successful investing, since it is necessary to use a multi-faceted approach in looking at investments, considering all the variables that could negatively or positively affect an investment. Also, creative thinking is required to look forward to the future and try to forecast the outcome of current business plans.

Be Independent

A number of successful investors have commented on the importance of independent and individual decision making. Sir John Templeton said, "If you buy the same securities as other people, you'll get the same results as other people." It is impossible to produce superior results unless one does something different from the majority.

Remain Flexible

It is important for investors to be flexible and not permanently adopt a particular type of asset. I think the best approach is to migrate from the popular to the unpopular securities or sectors. Flexibility is also an attribute that keeps one from holding on to a stock out of loyalty—flexibility allows one to change as times change and as new opportunities present themselves.

Investment Tools

So that's the personal preparation that goes into investing. On the professional side, it can't be stressed enough that in addition to meeting company managements and their competitors, it is important to be a voracious reader. A wide variety of reading contributes enormously to an investor's ability to make insightful decisions. Reading is like your body's muscles; use it or lose it. If you don't exercise regularly you will lose muscle tone and bone strength. If you don't read you will not be able to absorb new information and techniques.

Of course, there are also investment attitudes that will benefit your investment results. I'm going to use this space to list what I consider to be some of the most important investment rules I've picked up over the years.

Always Diversify Your Investments

Diversification is your best strategy to plan against unexpected events such as earthquakes, political upheaval, floods, investor panic, and the like—not only within a particular market, but also across markets globally. You never want to be overly dependent on the fate of any one stock or security, particularly if you don't have control over a company's management or events. Some successful investors with a limited number of holdings believe in the Mark Twain school of thought: "Put all your eggs in one basket—and watch that basket!" But these investors often have some influence on companies and management. Most investors are not able to do that, and if you fall into the latter category, you will always be better off diversifying across countries and companies. Global investing is always superior to investing in only your home market or one market. If you search worldwide, you will find more bargains and better bargains than by studying only one nation.

Don't Run from Risk

Without risk, I believe it is difficult for your portfolio to aim to achieve superior investment returns. But that risk taking is not the same as playing roulette or skydiving. The assumption of risk I'm talking about must be carefully planned and researched. Investment decisions always require decisions based on insufficient information. There is never enough time to learn all there is to know about an investment, as equity investments are undergoing continuous change. There comes a time when a decision must be made and a risk acquired. The ability to take just the right amount of risk based on the most diligently researched available information, in my mind, is the mark of a good investor.

Take a Long-Term View

Take a long-term view even if you desire short-term rewards. If you take a long-term view of the world and the markets, you are likely to (1) be less emotional and thus less likely to make costly mistakes; (2) see beyond the short-term volatility of the market; and (3) take a step back to see broader patterns of market, political, and economic behavior that may not be evident to a short-term observer. By looking at the long-term growth and prospects of companies and countries, particularly those stocks that are out of favor or unpopular, you will have a much greater chance of obtaining superior returns.

Make Volatility Your Friend

Markets are volatile, like a combustible material. You can warm up gasoline until a certain point, after which it ignites and explodes. But these market explosions give us an opportunity to buy low and sell high, as long as you have been wearing protective gear (such as diversification). The extreme sensitivity of markets to any news, what I call their "manic-depressive" nature, means that they often rise and fall by much more than they should. Remember that the time of maximum pessimism is the best time to buy and the point of maximum optimism is the best time to sell. If you can look beyond the emotional roller coaster of the volatility and use it to your advantage, you might be able do rather well on your investments.

Okay, you win some, you lose some—you can't avoid it. It's not only the name of the game, but the only game in town for emerging markets investors. However, some losses are not only avoidable but meaningful, because you learn lessons from them.

With just about every major loss we've incurred, we've picked up a few pointers. I try to avoid repeating the same mistakes again and again. Because, like most people, I hate being wrong too often, and I know that fund managers are only as good as their last performance.

We've had our fair share of losses, believe me. But at the end of the day, we must be ready to make mistakes; otherwise we would never learn. You might even say that hitting a few foul balls goes with the territory.

Even today, when the worst wounds have healed, the mere mention of some losers fills me with dread and regret, but, curiously, not anger—because any hard feelings are softened by the fact that we invariably learn from the experience.

As someone who's been punched by the markets more than once, I have some advice: Roll with the punches. If you're going to take real risks, you can't always count on rewards.

—————————————— ⁓ ——————————————

Roll with the punches. If you're going to take real risks, you can't always count on rewards.

If you follow the contrarian path, you're going to find yourself buying stock in distressed companies. You can't avoid it, because the vast majority of the bargains out there are in shares of organizations that have made a few mistakes along the way. That's why these stocks are so cheap. That's why a whole lot of smart people think they're headed nowhere in a hurry.

Our job is to prove them wrong. So how can we be so arrogant? Because we have the luxury, and the opportunity, of shifting our focus to a five-year time horizon. We can look ahead to a point out there in the distance where the long-term outlook may be more positive than the outlook in the short term. We also have the advantage of stacking the company up against other, similar companies elsewhere, often faced with similar challenges. Sometimes we can see an opportunity and some light where others see only darkness. And, of course, sometimes we're wrong.

We like finding good companies, and good countries, that have fallen on hard times, but only—we hope—temporarily; companies, and countries, poised to stage an unlikely comeback; companies, and countries, fighting an uphill battle to thrive, even to survive—because only when the odds are against you are you going to find any real bargains.

Those are your big winners. More often than not, the line separating the winners from the losers can be embarrassingly thin.

It's also important to recognize that not only is nobody perfect, but mistakes are an integral part of investing. You're never going to always pick winners, and picking losers—in my opinion—should in no way reflect any lack of care or negligence in the selection of investments for a portfolio under management.

These marvelous markets, as they continue to evolve and develop, may be volatile at times. But I sincerely hope that after reading this book, you'll no longer view volatility only in negative terms. Volatility can be a good thing for investors; be prepared to benefit from it. Market ups and downs, even the most violent ones, provide incentives for people to adapt to new environments and to shifting realities. Free markets can be harsh taskmasters, but to paraphrase what Winston Churchill once said of democracy, the free market may be a lousy system, but it just happens to be the best one we've got.

Acknowledgments

~

IF I WERE TO attempt to acknowledge all the wonderful people who helped formulate the ideas that went into this book, it would take many pages. Suffice it to say that I have learned a great deal from the thousands of people working in and studying emerging markets since I began this adventure in the 1970s even before I started managing the Templeton Emerging Markets Fund. Over the years, experts within the Franklin Resources organization have helped the Templeton Emerging Markets Group grow enormously in assets under management, and instead of five countries in which to invest in 1987 with only US\$100 million, we now cover more than 60 countries with over US\$50 billion invested.

Special thanks go to Shalini Dadlani for her excellent research and editing as well as the team at John Wiley & Sons who have helped bring this project to fruition. Of course I must take sole responsibility for any errors and omissions.

About the Author

Dr. Mark Mobius, Executive Chairman of Templeton Emerging Markets Group, joined Templeton in 1987 as managing director of its Far East Division in Hong Kong, with responsibility for supporting the Templeton Group's research expertise in emerging market countries. He directs the analysis for 17 global locations including Hong Kong, China, Singapore, Vietnam, India, South Korea, Malaysia, Thailand, United Arab Emirates, South Africa, Argentina, Brazil, Austria, Romania, Turkey, Poland, and Russia with a total of over US$50 billion under his supervision. Dr. Mobius has spent more than 40 years working in emerging markets and has extensive experience in economic research and analysis.

He has been named one of the "50 Most Influential
People" by *Bloomberg Markets* magazine, "Top 100 Most
Powerful and Influential People" by *Asiamoney* magazine,
"Emerging Markets Equity Manager" by International
Money Marketing, "Ten Top Money Managers of the
20th Century" by the Carson Group, "Investment Manager
of the Year" by the *Sunday Telegraph,* and "Closed-End
Fund Manager of the Year" by Morningstar. He holds a
Bachelor's and Master's degree from Boston University
and received his Ph.D. in Economics and Political Science
from Massachusetts Institute of Technology.

Dr. Mobius spends over 300 out of every 365 days
traveling around the world in search of the world's best
bargains.